The Complete Learn German For Adult

Beginners Book (3 in 1)

Master Reading, Writing, and Speaking German With This Simple 3 Step Process

Worldwide Nomad

Index

German Grammar Workbook and Textbook For Beginners

Introduction xi

Chapter 1.1 German Alphabet and Umlaute 1

Chapter 1.2 Noun classification, Articles, and Gender 7

Chapter 1.3 Grammatical Cases 11

Chapter 1.4 Pronouns 15

Chapter 1.5 Sentence Structuring 21

Chapter 1.6 Usage of Adjectives 25

Chapter 2.1 Overview of the Most Common Conjugation Rules 29

Chapter 2.2 Irregular Conjugation 35

Chapter 2.3 Modal Verbs and Their Conjugation 41

Chapter 2.4 Common Verbs and Their Conjugation 47

Chapter 3.1 Common Numbers 51

Chapter 3.2 Reading the Clock 55

Chapter 3.3 Systematic Construction of Big Numbers 59

Chapter 3.4 Fractions and Percentages 63

Chapter 4.1 Correct Usage of the Conjunctive Mood 67

Chapter 4.2 Constructing Compound Words 71

Chapter 4.3 Nuances of Prepositions 75

Chapter 4.4 Comma Placement 81

Chapter 4.5 Subordinate clauses 85

Chapter 4.6 Nonfinite verb forms 89

Chapter 4.7 Passive voice 93

Chapter 5.1 "False friend" terms for English speakers 97

Chapter 5.2 Hints for finding the right noun gender 103

Chapter 5.3 Common words with multiple connotations 107

Chapter 5.4 Getting negation right 111

Chapter 5.5 Tips for correct word ordering 115

Chapter 6.1 Job interviews 119

Chapter 6.2 Judicial system 123

Chapter 6.3 Party conversation and meeting new people 127

Chapter 6.4 Resolving verbal conflicts 131

Chapter 6.5 Haggling and negotiating.. 135

Chapter 6.6 Business meetings... 139

Chapter 7.1 Separable verbs.. 143

Chapter 7.2 When to use genitive or dative.. 147

Chapter 7.3 Difference between new and old spelling rules................................ 151

Answer key 155

German Phrasebook For Beginners

Introduction 165

Chapter 1 Greeting in German 169

    The Basics 170
    Express Politeness 171
    Be Mindful of Time.. 172
    Engage in Small Talk 173
    Use Formal Language 173
    Learn Basic Phrases in German 174
    Show Genuine Interest 174
    Participate in Cultural Customs 174

Chapter 2 Transportation 177

    Metros and Subways 179
    Taxis and Ride-Sharing Services.. 180
    Common Phrases and Vocabulary 180

Chapter 3 Accommodation, Hotels and Airbnb in Germany 185

    What to expect and what to offer? 186
    Now, let's learn! 186

Chapter 4 Food, Restaurants, and Cafés 193

Chapter 5 The Shopping Experience in German-Speaking Countries 201

Chapter 6 Drugstores and Hospital Visits in German-Speaking Countries 211

Chapter 7 What to avoid doing in Germany 221

Conclusion 225

German Short Stories For Language Learners

Das Wissenschaftliche Rätsel 229
The Scientific Conundrum 230
Vertrauen Mißbraucht 232
Betrayal 233
Der Chaos Säende Händler 235
The Chaos Sowing Merchant 236
Tapferkeit In Der Falschen Wendung 238
Bravery At The Wrong Turn 239
Der Heilige Römische Kaiser 241
The Holy Roman Emperor 242
Die Piraten Von Lazytown 244
The Pirates Of Lazytown 245
Die Krieger Des Friedens 247
The Warriors Of Peace 248
Das Machtgerangel 250
The Power Tussle 251
Liebe In Rauen Zeiten 253
Love In Harsh Times 254
Der Tag Der Mutter Celia 256
The Day Of Mother Celia 257
Franziskus Der Vornehme 259
Francis The Genteel 260
Der Deutsche Bundesstaat 262
The German Confederation 263
Helles Geister 265
Bright Minds 266
Bruderschaft 268
Brotherhood 269
Deutschland In Der Neuen Welt 271
Germany In The New World 272
Die Wahrheit Des Krieges 274

The Truth Of War 275

Braves Herz 277

Brave Heart 278

Das Licht In Unseren Herzen 280

The Light In Our Hearts 281

Zuhause Ist, Wo Das Herz Ist 283

Home Is Where The Heart Lies 284

Die Europäische Union 286

The European Union 287

Conclusion **289**

German Grammar Workbook and Textbook For

Beginners

Learn German With Essential, Easy to Understand Lessons

Worldwide Nomad

Introduction

As far as languages go, today's formalized version of German is relatively young. First attempts to create a common linguistic framework out of mutually intelligible, but sometimes overly idiosyncratic dialects with their own grammatical oddities began in the 18th century. Initially, this "high German" framework served as a means of communication for academics and other learned professions, but eventually percolated into everyday life.

Thanks to universal schooling, all Germans eventually familiarized themselves with it and could speak it, though distinctive regional dialects proliferate to this day, especially in Germany's south and east (as well as Austria and Switzerland). When learning German as a second language, you might be occasionally thrown off balance when dealing with local idioms of this kind, but don't worry: native German speakers face the same problem. It's a common theme in jokes and humor.

The evolution of German as a language is not yet finished. For instance, there was a recent spelling reform that changed the way compound words are constructed and limited the usage of the sharp S, the ß. There are still many people who stick to the old spelling though, and you'll learn some nuances of the old and new spelling system in chapter 7.4.

After completing the lessons in this booklet, you'll have a basic grasp on the fundamentals of German grammar, be able to construct sentences from scratch, and have some key phrases at your disposal to help you navigate everyday life. At the end of each chapter, there's a textbook-style quiz to test your newly acquired knowledge, with the answer key to these quizzes featured at the end of the booklet.

Now, without further ado, let's start your German language learning journey by looking at the most fundamental part of the language: the alphabet and its intricacies.

Chapter 1.1
German Alphabet and Umlaute

The German alphabet shares many similarities with the English alphabet. Both contain the 26 letters of the Standard English alphabet, though their pronunciation is sometimes very different. Here are the 26 common letters and their official German pronunciation, the way you would learn it in elementary school, spelled out for an English speaker:

A	ah
B	beh
C	tseh
D	deh
E	eh
F	eff
G	geh
H	ha
I	ee
J	yott
K	kah
L	ell
M	emm
N	enn
O	oh
P	peh
Q	coo
R	err
S	ess
T	teh
U	oo
V	fau
W	veh
X	ix
Y	ipsilon
Z	tsett

In contrast to English, where the same letter can have different pronunciations depending on the word (compare the spelling of "u" in "run" and "ruminate"), letter pronunciation in German is more forgiving and follows stable rules based on the alphabetical pronunciation, so you won't have to learn that many exceptions. There are some notable irregularities though:

The letter Q never stands on its own and is always followed by a U, the same way it is in English. As such, the alphabetical sound "coo" practically never comes up except in made-up names for products and suchlike. The pronunciation of "Qu" is the exact same as in English.

The alphabetical pronunciation of the letter Y ("ipsilon") only occurs when the letter is used as part of a hyphenated word, for example in "Y-Chromosom" (Y chromosome) or "y-Achse" (y-axis of a graph). In general, the letter is rarely used in contemporary German. In the past, it replaced the letter I in some spelling variants or dialects, but this has all been eliminated. You'll mostly find it as part of loan words now, in which case it is either pronounced as in "yell" (e.g. Yeti, Yoga) or as an Ü (Dynamik, Psychologie). We'll get to the Umlaute in a minute, don't worry. It can also occur as part of names (Yvonne, Sylvia), in which case it's pronounced the same as the German I ("ee") or the same way I is pronounced in "industry" or "India."

There are two different pronunciations for the German V. This is the one situation where you'll unfortunately have to simply remember the right variation for every single word. In the German word "Vase," the V is pronounced the same way as in the eponymous English term. In the word "Vier" (four), it's pronounced as an F. As a general rule, terms that are obvious loan words ("Veritabel," "Virus," "Verifizierung") use the English spelling of V while more natively Germanic terms ("Volk," "Vater," "voll") require the F spelling.

ß: The "sharp S"

Now let's get into the letters that German doesn't share with English. The more exotic-looking, but also easier one is ß. It only exists in lower case form since there are no words that start with it. If you find yourself capitalizing an entire word for whatever reason, you can replace the ß with two S, for example, STRASSE (street).

The pronunciation is easy and already apparent from the example above: "ss," a drawn-out or double S, basically. Try pronouncing it in the words "Straße," "Soße" (sauce) or "Gruß" (greeting). You probably got it right the first time around.

In Swiss German, the letter ß isn't used and is always replaced by two S in the respective words.

Umlaute: Ä, Ö, and Ü

These are the more challenging letters for English speakers since there are no native English pronunciations for Ü. Furthermore, all the Umlaute have two different versions, a short and a drawn-out one, which you'll have to once again remember for each individual word.

Let's get the easier of the two Umlaute out of the way: the short version of Ä is pronounced like the "a" in "apple." German examples of the short Ä would be "Männer" (men) or "Hänger" (trailer). Its long version is pronounced like the "ai" in "air" and is used in terms like "Mädchen" (girl) or "Fähre" (ferry).

The sound of the long Ö is similar to the "u" in "occur." German examples would be "hören" (hear) or "böse" (evil). The short Ö bears similarity to the way "i" is pronounced in "flirt" and needs to be employed in terms like "Töpfe" (pots) or "Löffel" (spoon).

There's no way to describe the pronunciation of Ü through comparison with an English word or letter. Instead, we have to be mechanical about it: produce the "ee" sound of the German I or the English I in "industry" and then close your lips almost, but not completely. Congratulations, you just spoke your first "Ü!"

The difference between long and short Ü only comes down to how long you make this sound. The short Ü is used to say "Müll" (trash) or "Fülle" (fullness). The long Ü, often but not always accompanied by an H, shows up in the terms "Mühle" (mill) or "Gefühl" (feeling).

Combination letters: "ch" and "sch"

You've now mastered all the individual letters of the German alphabet. As a last exercise of this chapter, you'll learn how to pronounce the commonly used letter combinations "ch" and "sch."

The "sch" compound is the easier of the two for an English speaker: It sounds the same as the "sh" in "fish" or "dish." Examples in German would be "Schule" (school) or "Schublade" (drawer).

"Ch" is trickier. It has two different pronunciation variants, one of which isn't native to the English language. The one native to English sounds like a "k" and is primarily used in names of locations or people, such as Chiemsee or Christoph.

The other variant is best described as a hissing sound, the kind a cat would make when upset or threatened. Another approximation would be an overly emphasized pronunciation of the "h" in "human,, basically pronouncing it as "chuman," but in a guttural way. This is the more common variant of the two, so you'll ill have to familiarize yourself with it. German examples include "ich" (I) and "dich" (accusative of "you"), so as you can see, you'll end up using it all the time.

Exercises

Remember the different pronunciations of Y and when they typically occur, then decide in which of the following words the letter Y is pronounced the same as in "you" or "yell":

1. a) Yucca   b) Yen
    c) Yvonne   d) Elektrolyse

2. a) Psychologie   b) Yacht
    c) Hyper   d) Yeti

Remember the short and long version of the Umlaute. Based on the rules you have learned, which of the following contains a long Umlaut:

3. a) Härte b) Tür
    c) Währung d) Möhre

4. a) Löffel b) Währung
    c) kränklich d) böse

Remember the two different versions of "ch". In which of the following terms is it pronounced as a "k" sound:

5. a) Christian b) mich
    c) sicher d) Chor

Chapter 1.2
Noun classification, Articles, and Gender

Unlike the English language, where most nouns don't have a gender, German nouns are always part of one of three grammatical genders: male, female, or neutral. This gender affects the article belonging to the word.

Let's start with a brief overview of the gendered **definite** articles:

	male	female	neutral
singular	DER Mann	DIE Frau	DAS Ding
plural	DIE Männer	DIE Frauen	DIE Dinge

As you can tell, die plural article of all three genders is "die," which makes it easier to remember. The singular article of female nouns is also "die." The only deviation occurs in male singular (der) and neutral singular (das).

Now let's examine gendered **indefinite** articles:

	male	female	neutral
singular	EIN Mann	EINE Frau	EIN Ding
plural	Männer	Frauen	Dinge

Only the singular forms of nouns have indefinite articles in German. Plural forms don't have them, just like in English. The indefinite article for male and neutral nouns is "ein," for female nouns it's "eine."

Unfortunately, there's no way to systematically categorize in your head what might be a male, female, or neutral noun. There really is no logic to it and you'll have to learn the correct gender for every single noun you encounter. This is typically something that takes German learners a long time to master, so don't feel discouraged if you mess up occasionally.

Capitalization

Only names and words at the start of a sentence are typically capitalized in English. In German, however, all nouns are capitalized, including nominalized verbs and adjectives.

Two example sentences illustrate the point:

The man followed the cat into the house.
Der Mann folgte der Katze in das Haus.

Ellen enjoys the beautiful and colorful.
Ellen genießt das Schöne und Bunte.

"Cat" is actually a female noun in German; the reason we used the article "der" in the example sentence is that these articles vary by grammatical case, too. But you'll learn more about that in the next chapter.

Declining nouns

Noun declination in German is quite random, follows no systematic distribution, and (this is becoming a theme at this point) you'll have to learn the correct declination for every word you use. It's a feature of the German language in many ways.

Here are the different types of singular/plural declination you will encounter:

No change

der Käfer / die Käfer (bug)
das Mädchen / die Mädchen (girl)

Some good news for you though: this declination doesn't occur in female nouns, so that's one less option for you to worry about when it comes to female nouns.

Vowel change

der Vater / die Väter (father)
die Mutter / die Mütter (mother)
das Kloster / die Klöster (monastery)

Added e

der Hund / die Hunde (dog)
die Mühsal / die Mühlsale (struggle)
das Schicksal / die Schicksale (fate)

Added n or en

der Fleck / die Flecken (stain)
die Frau / die Frauen (woman)
das Auge / die Augen (eye)

Added s

der Treff / die Treffs (hangout spot)
die Kamera / die Kameras (camera)

das Auto / die Autos (car)

Added er

der Geist / die Geister (ghost)
das Kind / die Kinder (child)
No female nouns use this variant.

Vowel change plus letter addition

der Zug / die Züge (train)
die Hand / die Hände (hand)
das Buch / die Bücher (book)

Rote memorization and routine use of the language is your best bet for figuring out which singular/plural declination to use.

Exercises

Recall the gendered definite and indefinite articles you learned in the beginning of the chapter. Which of these article pairs are correct:

1. a) der Baum / eine Baum   b) die Schule / eine Schule
    c) das Haus / ein Haus   d) das Tier / eine Tier

2. a) das Haus / einen Haus   b) die Hand / das Hände
    c) das Auto / die Autos   d) der Vater / die Väter

You learned about capitalization rules. If you were to translate the following sentence into German, which words would have to be capitalized: "We sat around the lake, listening to the sounds of the night and the singing of the birds."

3. a) lake, sounds, night   b) lake, sounds, night, birds
    c) lake, sounds, listening, night   d) lake, sounds, night, singing, birds

You learned about some examples for declining the plural form. Which ones are correct

4. a) das Mädchen / die Mädchener   b) der Hund / die Hünde
    c) das Auto / die Autoen   d) das Kind / die Kinder

5. a) das Schicksal / die Schicksale   b) die Mutter / die Muttere
    c) der Geist / die Geister   d) der Zug / die Zuger

Chapter 1.3
Grammatical Cases

German has four grammatical cases: nominative, genitive, dative, and accusative. English also uses the nominative and genitive cases, but employs different linguistic constructions for the other two. To differentiate the four cases, it's best to ask the simple question: who or what is being addressed?

Nominative: The dog loves his toys. *Who* loves his toys? The dog.
Genitive: The dog's toys look fancy. *Whose* toys look fancy? The dog's.
Dative: I gave the dog toys. *Whom* did you give toys? The dog.
Accusative: I can't keep the dog from his toys. *Who* can't you keep from his toys? The dog.

You can already tell from the example that English doesn't inflect words to construct the dative and accusative, but German does, and in irregular ways too. In addition to that, it changes definite and indefinite articles differently based on the **gender** of the noun, which you learned about in the previous chapter. At least here the rules are systematic and apply in every case.

This is how cases affect words and gendered articles in German:

	Nominative	Genitive	Dative	Accusative
Male	der Mann	des Mannes	dem Mann	den Mann
Female	die Frau	der Frau	der Frau	die Frau
Neutral	das Ding	des Dings	dem Ding	das Ding

For some words ending with a vowel, such as Löwe (lion, male), the word is being inflected irregularly to accommodate the cases. The declination for Löwe would be:

der Löwe, des Löwen, dem Löwen, den Löwen

Notice the contrast with "Mann" which is formed slightly differently. However, this isn't always the case; see the declination for the word Klasse (class, female):

die Klasse, der Klasse, der Klasse, die Klasse

This is another situation where the proper declination has to be learned and memorized for each word. Now let's investigate plural cases and their formation:

	Nominative	Genitive	Dative	Accusative
Male	die Männer	der Männer	den Männern	die Männer
Female	die Frauen	der Frauen	den Frauen	die Frauen
Neutral	die Dinge	der Dinge	den Dingen	die Dinge

For the sake of comparison, this is how "der Löwe" is inflected in its plural form:

die Löwen, der Löwen, den Löwen, die Löwen

With a bit of routine, you'll eventually figure out all the irregular words and inflect them correctly.

Here's what this declination looks like for indefinite articles:

	Nominative	Genitive	Dative	Accusative
Male	ein Mann	eines Mannes	einem Mann	einen Mann
Female	eine Frau	einer Frau	einer Frau	eine Frau
Neutral	ein Ding	eines Dings	einem Ding	ein Ding

Recall that plural forms of the indefinite articles don't exist in German. One less problem to keep track of!

Exercises

Which of these sentences contains a dative clause?

a) a) Tim gave snacks to his friend's dog.
    b) Our dog loves his snacks.
    c) Our friend's dog loves Tim.
    d) Tim's dog is healthy.

b) a) We arrived at the party late.
    b) The party had many guests.
    c) The party's guests had many snacks.
    d) The host greeted the guests.

Which of these article plus noun constructions are correct?

c) a) dem Mannes   b) eine Mann
    c) einen Mann   d) den Mann

d) a) der Ding   b) einen Ding
    c) ein Ding   d) das Ding

e) a) einer Frau   b) eine Frau
    c) der Frau   d) die Frau

Chapter 1.4
Pronouns

German has seven types of pronouns which are subject to specific inflection rules. In this chapter we'll go over the four most important categories that you'll use in practically any sentence and study how to use them properly.

Personal pronouns

I	ich
you	du
he	er
she	sie
it	es
we	wir
you (plural)	ihr
they	sie

Reflexive pronouns

oneself, themselves	sich

Possessive pronouns

my	mein
your	dein
his, its	sein
her	ihr
our	unser
your (plural)	euer

Relative pronouns

who	der, die, das
which	der, die, das
that	der, die, das

What you see above is the nominative inflection of these pronouns and they can obviously be inflected like nouns in general (except that the genitive case cannot be applied to them for logical reasons). The inflection of the personal pronouns looks as follows:

	Nominative	Accusative	Dative
singular I	ich	mich	mir
plural	wir	uns	uns
singular you	du	dich	dir
plural	ihr	euch	euch
singular he	er	ihn	ihm
plural	sie	sie	ihnen
singular she	sie	sie	ihr
plural	sie	sie	ihnen
singular it	es	es	ihm
plural	sie	sie	ihnen

Now, before your head starts spinning too much from all the inflections, let's construct some example sentences to see them in action.

He has made **me** very happy.
Er hat **mich** sehr glücklich gemacht.

I have promised **him** much.
Ich habe **ihm** viel versprochen.

I have made lunch for **myself**.
Ich habe **mir** Mittagessen gemacht.

She hasn't heard **it** yet.
Sie hat **es** noch nicht gehört.

We will invite **them** for dinner.
Wir werden **sie** zum Abendessen einladen.

Note that, because the plural forms of "er," "sie," and "es" are identical, you can simply use "sie" and "ihnen" for all groups of people and objects regardless of the gender of their individual members.

There's also a formal "you" in German similar to the Spanish "usted." In the second person singular and plural, you can and should use the personal pronoun "**Sie**" when addressing authority figures or people you don't know.

The inflection of the reflexive pronoun "sich" is always "sich."

They have built **themselves** a house.
Sie haben **sich** ein Haus gebaut.

The inflection of the possessive pronouns works like this:

	Nominative	Accusative	Dative
singular my	mein(e)	meine(n)	meinem(r)
plural	unser(e)	unsere(n)	unserem(r)
singular your	dein(e)	deine(n)	deinem(r)
plural	euer(eure)	eure(n)	eurem(r)
singular his	sein(e)	seine(n)	seinem(r)
plural	ihr(e)	ihre(n)	ihrem(r)
singular her	ihr(e)	ihre(n)	ihrem(r)
plural	ihr(e)	ihre(n)	ihrer
singular its	sein(e)	seine(n)	seinem(r)
plural	ihr(e)	ihre(n)	ihrem(r)

The bracketed (e), (n) and (r) at the end of some inflections indicate different spellings for different noun genders. Female nouns require the additional e and the variant r spelling; male nouns require the additional n:

My father owns **his** own house.
Mein Vater besitzt **sein** eigenes Haus.

Our mother owns **her** own home.
Unsere Mutter besitzt **ihr** eigenes Haus.

Your cats look cute in **their** cat corner.
Deine Katzen sehen süß aus in **ihrer** Katzenecke.

I have met **your** father today.
Ich habe heute **deinen** Vater getroffen.

Let us finally take a look at the inflection of the relative pronouns:

	Nominative	Genitive	Accusative	Dative
who, which, that	der, die, das	dessen, deren, dessen	den, die, das	dem, der, dem
plural	die	deren	die	denen

To avoid confusion here: the English terms "who," "which," and "that" all mean the same thing in German; the three translations you see in the German brackets refer to the **gendered** version of each grammatical case (male, female, neutral).

The man **who** visits me often is my grandfather.
Der Mann, **der** mich oft besucht, ist mein Großvater.

The woman **that** visits me often is my grandmother.
Die Frau, **die** mich oft besucht, ist meine Großmutter.

The things **which** I observe on the street are funny.
Die Dinge, **die** ich auf der Straße sehe, sind witzig.

Despite the seemingly overwhelming number of pronouns in German, they're actually one of the easier concepts to learn and apply.

Exercises

Let's check your pronouns. Name the right German pronouns to be inserted into the following sentences

1. "**I** am doing **my** homework; then I will take **our** dog for a walk in **her** favorite park."
   a) Ich, deine, unseren, sie
   b) Ich, meine, unseren, ihrem
   c) es, meine, unseren, ihrem
   d) ich, meine, eurem, ihrem

2. "**Wir** sind froh über **euren** Besuch und hoffen, **es** gefällt **euch**."
   a) we, our, it, you
   b) we, your, he, your
   c) we, your, it, you
   d) us, our, it, you

3. "**Du** hast **sie** schon gesehen. **Ihnen** war kalt."
   a) your, them, they
   b) you, them, they
   c) our, them, they
   d) you, they, they

Recall your knowledge of relative pronouns and find the right ones for this sentence:

4. "My father, **who** works a lot, talked about his boss, **whom** he really likes."
   a) der, die
   b) den, den
   c) der, den
   d) der, der

5.　"Our house, **which** is very old, has many aspects **that** I really like."
　　a) der, die
　　b) das, die
　　c) der, das
　　d) das, denen

Chapter 1.5
Sentence Structuring

Much like the English language, the German language follows the subject-verb-object order as a general rule, meaning there are predetermined positions in a sentence for each part. It also adheres to the verb second rule which states that finite verbs must always occupy the second position in a sentence. While this ordering can be altered for purposes of emphasizing a particular word or part of the sentence, it's mostly used for artistic purposes.

Let's look at some example sentences:

Peter donated some clothes.
Peter verschenkte einige Klamotten.

Both sentences start with the subject, followed by the verb, followed by the object. Not much can be changed here in either language. But here's what we can do if we add some complexity to the sentence:

Peter donated some clothes to charity.
Peter spendete einige Klamotten an die Wohlfahrt.

Now we can restructure the sentence to put an emphasis on the dative object:

In support of charity, Peter donated some clothes.
An die Wohlfahrt spendete Peter einige Klamotten.

A key difference in sentence structure between German and English is the positioning of the verb in subordinate clauses:

Peter, who supports charity, donated some clothes.
Peter, der die Wohlfahrt unterstützt, spendete einige Klamotten.

In German, the verb in subordinate clauses always comes **last**. It's possible to mix this up for lyrical purposes, but in standard German writing and speaking, this would look and sound very much out of order. It applies to all kinds of subordinate clauses, too:

Peter donated some clothes because he supports charity.
Peter spendete einige Klamotten, weil er die Wohlfahrt unterstützt.

A related rule exists for interrogative clauses; the verb in this case has to come in **first**:

Does Peter donate clothes to charity?
Spendet Peter Klamotten an die Wohlfahrt?

We can switch the position of the subject and verb in this sentence to put emphasis on Peter: "Peter spendet Klamotten an die Wohlfahrt?" This would indicate surprise that Peter is doing this, whereas the previous sentence merely expressed a dispassionate interest in Peter's donation habits.

There are some notable differences in sentence structuring once we introduce additional or auxiliary verbs:

Peter supports donating clothes to charity and likes to donate often.
Peter unterstützt das Spenden an die Wohlfahrt und spendet gern regelmäßig.

As you can see, the second verb construction from the English sentence (donating) actually becomes a noun in German; whereas the verb "likes" becomes an adverb (gern) in German.

You'll learn more about that in the verb section of this booklet. This section was only meant to familiarize yourself with the basic sentence structuring of the German language.

Exercises

Rearrange these scrambled German sentences to make sure all the words are in their correct spot again:

1. "Klamotten Peter an die Wohlfahrt spendete, weil die Wohlfahrt unterstützt er."
   a) Peter an die Wohlfahrt spendete Klamotten, weil die Wohlfahrt er unterstützt.
   b) Peter spendete Klamotten an die Wohlfahrt, weil die Wohlfahrt er unterstützt.
   c) Peter spendete Klamotten an die Wohlfahrt, weil unterstützt er die Wohlfahrt.
   d) Peter spendete Klamotten an die Wohlfahrt, weil er die Wohlfahrt unterstützt.

2. "Peter Hat ein Auto großes?"
   a) Ein Auto großes hat Peter?
   b) Hat Peter ein großes Auto?
   c) Auto ein großes hat Peter?
   d) Peter hat ein großes Auto?

3. "Peter ein Auto großes hat der Klamotten einige spendete"
   a) Peter, der ein großes Auto hat, spendete einige Klamotten.
   b) Peter, ein großes Auto der hat, spendete einige Klamotten.
   c) Peter spendete einige Klamotten, der ein großes Auto hat.
   d) Peter, hat der ein großes Auto, spendete einige Klamotten.

Are the following true or false?

4. Two complete, non-modal verbs can occur right next to each other in German as full verbs.
   a) true
   b) false

5. The sentence structure in German can be rearranged at will to put emphasis on certain elements.
   a) true
   b) false

Chapter 1.6
Usage of Adjectives

Much like the pronouns you already learned about, adjectives in German are inflected according to the case and gender of the noun they accompany. Fortunately, the inflection of the positive (normal) form of German adjectives is regular and follows systematic patterns, with irregularities only occurring in the comparative and superlative forms.

There are two different inflections of adjectives in their positive form; one for situations where they are accompanied by an indefinite or no article and one for situations with a definite article.

Let's examine the difference via the adjective "gut" (good) by starting with the definite article inflection:

	Nominative	Genitive	Dative	Accusative
der (m.)	gute	guten	guten	guten
die (f.)	gute	guten	guten	gute
das (n.)	gute	guten	guten	gute
die (pl.)	guten	guten	guten	guten

Now compare the indefinite/no article inflection:

	Nominative	Genitive	Dative	Accusative
ein (m.)	guter	guten	guten	guten
eine (f.)	gute	guten	guten	gute
ein (n.)	gutes	guten	guten	gutes
(pl.)	gute	guter	guten	guten

In the specific scenario of a **dative singular case** with **no article**, the last letter "n" is replaced by "m" (for masculine and neutral genders) or "r" (for the feminine gender): "gutem," "guter."

In the subsection on definite and indefinite articles, you familiarized yourself with the gendered articles in their nominative version. But these articles need to be inflected to fit the case and gender of their respective nouns as well. Adjectives provide a great opportunity to learn about both at the same time, starting with the inflection of a definite article adjective construction:

Der gute Mann. **Des** guten Mannes. **Dem** guten Mann. **Den** guten Mann.

Die gute Frau. **Der** guten Frau. **Der** guten Frau. **Die** gute Frau.

Das gute Auto. **Des** guten Autos. **Dem** guten Auto. **Das** gute Auto.

Die guten Hunde. **Der** guten Hunde. **Den** guten Hunden. **Die** guten Hunde.

And once again for the indefinite article:

Ein guter Mann. **Eines** guten Mannes. **Einem** guten Mann. **Einen** guten Mann.

Eine gute Frau. **Einer** guten Frau. **Einer** guten Frau. **Eine** gute Frau.

Ein gutes Auto. **Eines** guten Autos. **Einem** guten Auto. **Ein** gutes Auto.

And finally, two examples of a dative singular case construction with no article:

Ich gehe mit groß**er** Freude (f.) zur Schule.
I attend school with great joy.

Ich gehe mit groß**em** Elan (m.) zur Schule.
I attend school with great enthusiasm.

That's all you need to know about the positive adjective form in German. When it comes to comparative and superlative forms, you'll once again have to do a bit of memorizing of the irregular inflections of certain adjectives. Before we get into the irregular ones, let's examine the comparative and superlative inflection of the regular German adjective "klein" (small):

comparative	Nominative	Genitive	Dative	Accusative
der (m.)	kleinere	kleineren	kleineren	kleineren
die (f.)	kleinere	kleineren	kleineren	kleinere
das (n.)	kleinere	kleineren	kleineren	kleinere
die (pl.)	kleineren	kleineren	kleineren	kleineren

comparative	Nominative	Genitive	Dative	Accusative
ein (m.)	kleinerer	kleineren	kleineren	kleineren
eine (f.)	kleinere	kleineren	kleineren	kleinere
ein (n.)	kleineres	kleineren	kleineren	kleineres
(pl.)	kleinere	kleinerer	kleineren	kleinere

superlative	Nominative	Genitive	Dative	Accusative
der (m.)	kleinste	kleinsten	kleinsten	kleinsten
die (f.)	kleinste	kleinsten	kleinsten	kleinste
das (n.)	kleinste	kleinsten	kleinsten	kleinste
die (pl.)	kleinsten	kleinsten	kleinsten	kleinsten

superlative	Nominative	Genitive	Dative	Accusative
ein (m.)	kleinster	kleinsten	kleinsten	kleinsten

eine (f.)	kleinste	kleinsten	kleinsten	kleinste
ein (n.)	kleinstes	kleinsten	kleinsten	kleinstes
(pl.)	kleinste	kleinsten	kleinsten	kleinste

Notable exceptions to this rule include:

- Commonly used and linguistically archaic adjectives such as "gut," which transforms into "besser" and "am besten," or "viel" (much), which transforms into "mehr" and "am meisten." Laying out the inflections for all these irregular verbs would overextend the limits of this basic chapter.
- A group of adjectives that inflect with an additional vowel change, for example "lang" (long) into "länger" and "am längsten" or "kurz" (short) into "kürzer" and "am kürzesten."
- Another group of adjectives that inflect with an additional vowel change **and** the addition of another letter, such as "nah" (near) into "näher" and "am nächsten" or "hoch" (high) into "höher" and "am höchsten."

While you certainly want to learn all the exceptions and irregularities correctly, rest assured that Germans will at least understand what you're saying even if you use wrong inflections like "guteste" or "höhste." In fact, this might serve as a humorous conversation starter.

Exercises

Which of the following adjective constructions is correct?

1. a) der gute Hund   b) der guten Frau
   c) die kleinstere Frau   d) ein kleinerer Hund

2. a) das guter Haus   b) dem guten Haus
   c) das kleinere Haus   d) dem kleineren Haus

3. a) der kleine Mann   b) die kleine Mann
   c) die kleinen Mann   d) die kleinen Männer

Build the comparative form for the regular German adjective "schön".

4. a) schönste   b) schöne
   c) schönster   d) schöner

Build the superlative for the regular adjective "breit".

5. a) breitstere   b) breiter
   c) breitester   d) breitst

Chapter 2.1
Overview of the Most Common Conjugation Rules

This chapter will no doubt remind you a lot of the last one: There's a basic way to conjugate German verbs that applies to most of them, and then there's the usual amount of irregular forms to learn and memorize. In this subchapter, you'll learn how to conjugate regular German verbs in their **present**, **simple future** and **past tense** form. There are more tenses than that in the German language, but those are reserved for the more advanced chapters.

Regular conjugation in the present tense

Let's use the regular German verb "machen" (make) to illustrate this conjugation:

ich	mache
du	machst
er, sie, es	macht
wir	machen
ihr	macht
sie	machen

There are a group of verbs, including "fahren" (drive) or "braten" (fry) that follow this pattern almost identically except for a vowel change in the second and third person singular:

ich	fahre
du	fährst
er, sie, es	fährt
wir	fahren
ihr	fahrt
sie	fahren

Two example sentences:

Sie **machen** sich Frühstück.
They are making breakfast for themselves.

Er **fährt** nach Berlin
He drives to Berlin.

Regular conjugation in the past tense

Again, we will use "machen" to illustrate this:

ich	machte
du	machtest
er, sie, es	machte
wir	machten
ihr	machtet
sie	machten

Unfortunately, the (in the present tense) almost regular group of verbs like "fahren" really starts to diverge a lot here:

ich	fuhr
du	fuhrst
er, sie, es	fuhr
wir	fuhren
ihr	fuhrt
sie	fuhren

To make matters worse, not all verbs from this group even use the same irregular past tense conjugation. Here's what "braten" looks like:

ich	briet
du	brietst
er, sie, es	briet
wir	brieten
ihr	brietet
sie	brieten

You'll learn about some more common examples of this kind of verb and how they're conjugated in chapter 2.4. For now, let's construct some sentences with our newfound knowledge:

Wir **machten** uns ein Ei zum Frühstück.
Wir made us an egg for breakfast.

Sie **fuhren** mit dem Zug.
They rode the train.

Regular conjugation in the simple future tense

This one tends to be more regular and predictable again. German uses the auxiliary verb "werden" (will) to construct this tense:

ich	werde machen
du	wirst machen
er, sie, es	wird machen
wir	werden machen
ihr	werdet machen
sie	werden machen

As you can see, we only conjugate the verb "werden" here and leave the other verb sitting next to it in its infinitive form. This is how the simple future tense works for all verbs in German. As long as you can conjugate "warden," you're all set!

A last batch of example sentences:

Wir **werden** Urlaub in Amerika **machen**.
We will go on vacation in America.

Ich **werde** nach München **fahren**.
I will drive to Munich.

Notice how the modal verb "werden" occupies the place of the verb in the regular sentence structure, with the actual verb relegated to the end of the sentence. You'll learn more about the placement of modal verbs in Chapter 2.3.

Exercises

Apply your knowledge of regular verb conjugation in the present tense and answer which of these present tense forms of "leben" are correct:

1. a) ich lebe   b) du lebt
    c) er lebte   d) du lebst

2. a) ihr leben   b) ihr lebt
    c) wir leben   d) sie leben

Which of these simple past forms of "leben" are correct?

3. a) ich lebte   b) du lebten
    c) sie lebte   d) wir lebten

4. a) du lebtest   b) ihr lebten
    c) sie lebten   d) es lebtet

Which of these simple future tense forms of "leben" are correct?

5. a) ich werden leben   b) sie werdet leben
    c) du wirst leben   d) ihr werdet leben

Chapter 2.2
Irregular Conjugation

Like most languages, irregular verb conjugation in German principally affects basic and original terms like "sein" (be) or "haben" (have), which unfortunately also means it's indispensable for you to memorize them since they come up all the time!

Let's start with the present tense conjugation of "sein":

ich	bin
du	bist
er, sie, es	ist
wir	sind
ihr	seid
sie	sind

And now the simple past tense:

ich	war
du	warst
er, sie, es	war
wir	waren
ihr	wart
sie	waren

Of course, the simple future is constructed in the same way you learned in the last chapter: "ich werde sein" and so on.

Once you get the hang of it, it's easy to apply this conjugated verb in example sentences:

Wir **sind** auf dem Weg nach Hause.
We are on our way home.

Sie **waren** mit mir im Restaurant.
They were in the restaurant with me.

Sie **wird** bald in Berlin **sein**.
She will be in Berlin soon.

With "sein" out of the way, we shall move on to "haben":

ich	habe
du	hast
er, sie, es	hat

wir	haben
ihr	habt
sie	haben

Past tense:

ich	hatte
du	hattest
er, sie, es	hatte
wir	hatten
ihr	hattet
sie	hatten

As you can see, the irregularity mostly comes in with past tense forms. Here are some more example sentences:

Du **hast** ein schönes Haus.
You have a beautiful house.

Wir **hatten** viel Spaß im Urlaub.
We had much fun on vacation.

Ihr **werdet** bald viel Arbeit **haben**.
You will have a lot of work soon.

Our third and last example of an irregular conjugation in this subchapter involves the word "wollen" (want), which, unlike "haben," is most irregular in its present tense:

ich	will
du	willst
er, sie, es	will
wir	wollen
ihr	wollt
sie	wollen

Not much going on in the past tense here:

ich	wollte
du	wolltest
er, sie, es	wollte

wir	wollten
ihr	wolltet
sie	wollten

And our last batch of examples for this subchapter:

Er **will** in unserer Firma anfangen.
He wants to join our company.

Wir **wollten** ein Haus mit Meerblick.
We wanted a house with a seaside view.

Sie **wird** bald nach neuen Aufgaben fragen **wollen**.
She will soon want to ask for new tasks.

As you may have noticed from the last example sentence, the simple future tense of "wollen" sounds a bit awkward in both German and English. For that reason, it's best to stick to the present tense since "wollen"/"want" already indicates a future orientation.

Exercises

Identify all the wrongly conjugated verbs in the following sentences:

1. "Ich bin auf dem Weg nach Berlin. Dort wollten ich meine Freunde treffen. Wir sein gute Freunde und hattest schon viel Spaß zusammen."
   a) bin, hattest
   b) wollten, sein
   c) wollten, sein, hattest
   d) bin, sein, hattest

2. "Wir werdet nach Berlin fahren. In Berlin wollen wir ein Restaurant besuchen. Es sind ein sehr gutes Restaurant."
   a) werdet, sind
   b) werdet, wollen
   c) werdet, wollen, sind
   d) sind

Construct the second person plural, past tense form of "wollen".

3. a) wolltet   b) wollten
   c) wollte   d) wolltest

Construct the first person singular, past tense form of "haben".

4. a) habet   b) hattet
    c) hatte   d) hatten

Which of those present tense forms of "haben" are correct?

5. a) ich habe   b) du habst
    c) wir haben   d) sie haben

Chapter 2.3
Modal Verbs and Their Conjugation

Modal verbs typically require the presence of another verb to function. There are altogether six modal verbs in German. You've already familiarized yourself with "wollen" (want) in the previous subchapter. The other five modal verbs are as follows:

sollen (shall)
können (can)
dürfen (may)
mögen (like)
müssen (must)

The presence of a modal verb changes the sentence structure, with the full verb that is assisted by the modal verb placed at the end of the sentence and the modal verb occupying its place as the second part of the sentence. For example:

Ich **gehe** nach München.
I go to Munich.

Ich **will** nach München **gehen**.
I want to go to Munich.

Modal verbs typically require the full verb to be used in an infinitive state ("gehen").

In colloquial German, it's possible to leave out the full verb that accompanies the modal verb if it's obvious what is being said, though it's not advisable to do this in formal writing:

Can you speak English?
Kannst du Englisch (**sprechen**)?

All modal verbs have irregular conjugations and we'll now briefly go over the details for the other five modal verbs besides "wollen." We'll begin the overview with "sollen." The first form in the right column is the present tense, the second is the past tense:

ich	soll, sollte
du	sollst, solltest
er, sie, es	soll, sollte
wir	sollen, sollten
ihr	sollt, solltet
sie	sollen, sollten

Ich **soll** nach München gehen.
I shall/am supposed to go to Munich.

Wir **sollen** weniger Lärm machen.
We shall/are supposed to make less noise.

"Können"

ich	kann, konnte
du	kannst, konntest
er, sie, es	kann, konnte
wir	können, konnten
ihr	könnt, konntet
sie	können, konnten

Er **konnte** seinen Zug noch erreichen.
He could still catch his train.

Wir **können** bald in unsere Wohnung einziehen.
We can soon move into our apartment.

"Dürfen"

ich	darf, durfte
du	darfst, durftest
er, sie, es	darf, durfte
wir	dürfen, durften
ihr	dürft, durftet
sie	dürfen, durften

Ihr **dürft** bei uns übernachten.
You may spend the night at our place.

Sie **durfte** bei der Prüfung keinen Taschenrechner benutzen.
She wasn't allowed to use a calculator for her exam.

"Mögen"

ich	mag, mochte
du	magst, mochtest
er, sie, es	mag, mochte
wir	mögen, mochten

ihr	mögt, mochtet
sie	mögen, mochten

Ich **mag** gern Eiscreme essen.
I like to eat ice cream.

Er **mochte** heute Abend nicht mehr vorbeikommen.
He didn't want to stop by anymore this evening.

"Müssen"

ich	soll, sollte
du	sollst, solltest
er, sie, es	soll, sollte
wir	sollen, sollten
ihr	sollt, solltet
sie	sollen, sollten

Sie **müssen** bald aus ihrer Wohnung ausziehen.
They need to leave their apartment soon.

Ich **musste** später beim Professor nachfragen.
I had to ask the professor later.

Exercises

Identify the correctly conjugated modal verbs in these sentences:

1. "Ich kann heute nicht kommen. Wir müsstet noch länger arbeiten. Aber ich mag morgen kommen und ich darfst das dann auch."
    a) müsstet, mag
    b) kann, mag
    c) müsstet, darfst
    d) kann, mag, darfst

2. "Wir dürfen meinen Vater besuchen. Vorher sollen wir aber noch den Hund holen, denn mein Vater kann das heute nicht."
    a) dürfen, sollen, kann
    b) dürfen
    c) dürfen, sollen
    d) kann

Construct the third person plural, past tense forms of "dürfen":

3. a) sie dürften   b) sie durften
    c) sie durfte   d) sie durftet

Which of those are correct combinations of pronouns and verbal forms?

4. a) wir mögen   b) sie mögen
    c) ich mögte   d) er mag

5. a) ich soll   b) wir sollten
    c) ihr solltet   d) du sollst

Chapter 2.4
Common Verbs and Their Conjugation

ou learned in Chapter 2.1 that a number of common German verbs have almost, but not totally regular conjugations. In this chapter we'll discover some examples of these and how they're properly conjugated.

"Geben" (give)

ich	gebe, gab
du	gibst, gabst
er, sie, es	gibt, gab
wir	geben, gaben
ihr	gebt, gabt
sie	geben, gaben

Sie **gab** ihrem Vorgesetzten die fertigen Unterlagen.
She gave the finished documents to her supervisor.
Wir **geben** heute bei der Prüfung unser Bestes.
or
Wir **werden** heute bei der Prüfung unser Bestes **geben**.
At today's exam, we will give our best.

"Sehen" (see)

ich	sehe, sah
du	siehst, sahst
er, sie, es	sieht, sah
wir	sehen, sahen
ihr	seht, saht
sie	sehen, sahen

Ich **sehe** mich nach einer neuen Wohnung um.
I'm looking for a new apartment.

Zuletzt **sahen** wir ihn am Montag.
We last saw him on Monday.

"Gehen" (go, walk)

ich	gehe, ging
du	gehst, gingst
er, sie, es	geht, ging

wir	gehen, gingen
ihr	geht, gingt
sie	gehen, gingen

Sie **ging** von der Bar nach Hause.
She went home from the bar.

Ich **gehe** dabei ein großes Risiko ein.
I am taking a big risk with this.

As you can see, there isn't really a pattern with these irregular verbs. Some have unusual forms that you'll just have to get acquainted with. Fortunately, because they're so common and you hear and use them all the time, you'll surely memorize all the correct irregular forms quickly!

Exercises

Which of the following verbs is conjugated correctly?

1. a) wir seht   b) ich ging
   c) er gabt   d) sie gibt

2. a) du sahst   b) sie sah
   c) er sahen   d) er sah

3. a) du gabt   b) wir gaben
   c) sie ging   d) es ging

You have learned two other German non-modal verbs with slightly irregular conjugation so far. Identify their correct forms:

4. a) sie briet   b) wir brieten
   c) ihr briet   d) es brätet

5. a) er fährt   b) ihr fuhrt
   c) sie fuhren   d) wir fuhrt

Chapter 3.1
Common Numbers

After spending all this time on words and grammar, let's have a change of pace and to delve into the topic of numbers in the German language: What they're called, how the more difficult ones are constructed, and some practical applications, like reading the clock or expressing simple mathematical concepts in German.

The basics

Let's start by giving names to simple numbers:

1 = Eins	2 = Zwei	3 = Drei	4 = Vier	5 = Fünf	6 = Sechs
7 = Sieben	8 = Acht	9 = Neun	10 = Zehn	11 = Elf	12 = Zwölf

Hopefully you studied your Umlaute so you can pronounce all of them correctly! The letters 13 to 19 follow a fairly simple linguistic pattern:

13 = Dreizehn	14 = Vierzehn	15 = Fünfzehn	16 = Sechzehn
17 = Siebzehn	18 = Achtzehn	19 = Neunzehn	

From 20 onward, a systematic counting system is used that is easy to memorize as long as you know the German terms for the decimal numbers:

20 = Zwanzig	21 = Einundzwanzig	22 = Zweiundzwanzig
23 = Dreiundzwanzig	…	29 = Neunundzwanzig

Simply start with the German name of the second digit, add "und" (meaning "and"), and then add the name of the decimal number. The only irregularity is that "Eins" turns into "Ein."

Here are the names of the other decimals:

30 = Dreißig	40 = Vierzig	50 = Fünfzig	60 = Sechzig
70 = Siebzig	80 = Achtzig	90 = Neunzig	

You'll learn about constructing bigger numbers than those in Chapter 3.3. For now, try pronouncing and memorizing the small numbers; they tend to come up a lot!

Making use of numbers

Now let's consider some practical applications. Imagine you're at the market and you want to know about the price of a product.

"How much is this?"
"Wie viel kostet das?"

The response might be:

"**Drei** Euro" or "**Drei** Euro **Fünfzehn,**" indicating that this product costs €3,15.

If someone asks about your age, the correctly phrased response would be:

"Ich bin **dreißig** Jahre alt."
"I am 30 years old."

You might want to inquire or say something about a certain date of the year. Dates in Germany are constructed by means of DD.MM.YYYY. For example, 15.04.1985. But how do you pronounce the date? Counted numbers like "fifteenth" from our example work like this in German:

1st = Erster	2nd = Zweiter	3rd = Dritter	4th = Vierter
...	19th = Neunzehnter	20th = Zwanzigster	

Keep in mind that those are adjectives subject to the same inflection by grammatical gender and case that you've learned about in previous chapters.

Heute ist der **zweite** Januar.
Today is January 2nd.

Dies ist schon mein **dritter** Versuch.
This is my third attempt already.

Exercises

Which of the following German dates are spelled out correctly?

1. a) dreizehnter Juli   b) siebenzehnter Juli
    c) erste Juli   d) siebter Juli

2. a) dreißigster Mai   b) zehner Mai
    c) vierundzwanzig Mai d) elfter Mai

Which of the following terms correctly describes a price in German?

3. a) "Fünf zehn Euro"   b) "Euro Sieben Siebzehn"
    c) "Acht Euro neun"   d) "Zehn Euro siebzehn"

4. a) "Fünfundzwanzig Euro" b) "Zwanzig Euro zwanzig"
    c) "Neunter Euro"   d) "Neun Euro neunzehnter"

5. a) "Achtzig Euro"   b) "Achtzig Euro achtachtzig"
    c) "Achtzige Euro achtzig" d) "Achtzigacht Euro"

Chapter 3.2
Reading the Clock

The basic statement of time in German that corresponds to "It is X o'clock" in English is "Es ist X Uhr." Unlike colloquial English, which generally operates with a 12-hour clock framework that resets at noon, the German language uses all 24 hours of the day.

"Es ist **acht Uhr**"
"Es ist **dreiundzwanzig Uhr**"

If you want to add minutes to your time statements, simply attach the minute number:

"Es ist **acht Uhr zwanzig**."

Some Germans also express minutes by counting how many have passed since the turn of the hour. Alternatively, if there are fewer than 30 minutes left of the hour, how long it is until the next hour.

"Es ist **zwanzig nach acht**."
"It is 20 past 8."

"Es ist **zwanzig vor acht**."
"It is 20 before 8."

German also has a variety of expressions to delineate the 15, 30, and 45-minute marks. For instance, 8:15 could be:

"Es ist **Viertel nach acht**."
"It is quarter past 8."

or:

"Es ist **Viertel neun**."
"It is quarter to 9."

For telling the half hour mark, there's only this expression; note that the time referenced here is the next hour, not the previous one like in English:

"Es ist **halb neun**."
"It is half past 8."

And lastly, for the 45-minute mark, there are once again two expressions:

"Es ist **Dreiviertel neun**."
"It is three quarters to 9."

or:

"Es ist **Viertel vor neun**."
"It is a quarter before 9."

Maybe you forget your watch or phone one day and would like to ask a stranger for the time. The direct question would be:

"**Wie viel Uhr ist es**?"
"What time is it?"

However, that would be quite direct and you should only use this phrase with people you're familiar with or have already conversed with. A more polite phrase would be:

"Könnten Sie mir bitte sagen, **wie viel Uhr es ist**?"
"Could you please tell me what time it is?"

If you want to express to someone that you wish to meet in X minutes or hours, the phrasing is exactly the same as in English:

"Lass uns **in 2 Stunden** treffen."
"Let us meet in 2 hours."

Exercises

1. Spell out in German the two special ways to say "3:45 o'clock".
    a) Viertel vier, Dreiviertel vier
    b) Dreiviertel drei, viertel vier
    c) Dreiviertel vier, Viertel vor vier
    d) Viertel vor drei, dreiviertel vier

Which of the following statements of time is not a proper German idiom?

2. a) Dreizehn vor sieben   b) Vierzig vor neun
    c) Halb zwölf   c) Halb vor drei

3. a) Sieben Uhr sechs   b) Viertel nach drei
    c) Neunzehn Uhr   d) Achtzehnte Uhr

4. a) Siebzehn Uhr halb   b) Halb sieben
    c) Sieben halb   d) Sieben Uhr dreißig

Is this true or false: Germans count their time in 12-hour intervals?

5. a) true   b) false

Chapter 3.3
Systematic Construction
of Big Numbers

Y ou already learned in Chapter 3.1 how to construct smaller numbers up to 99. Now you'll learn to count the big ones too, just in case you're lucky enough to win the German lottery!

100 = hundert / einhundert   200 = zweihundert   300 = dreihundert
…   900 = neunhundert

To construct numbers between the individual hundreds, simply add the name of the number in the last two digits to the end of the hundred.

115 = hundertfünfzehn   372 = dreihundertzweiundsiebzig
405 = vierhundertfünf   520 = fünfhundertzwanzig

Now let's repeat this exercise for the category of thousands:

1.000 = tausend / eintausend 2.000 = zweitausend   3000 = dreitausend
15.000 = fünfzehntausend   500.000 = fünfhunderttausend

The same system from the "hundreds category" also applies here:

153.256 = hundertdreiundfünfzigtausendzweihundertsechsundzwanzig

Typically, Germans don't spell out those numbers for obvious reasons. But if you find yourself in a situation where you have to say a number like that, that's what it sounds like!

It works exactly the same with numbers of one million and above, but do keep in mind that German uses slightly different terminology for some of those big numbers:

a million = eine Million   a billion = eine **Milliarde**
a trillion = eine **Billion**

1.500.062 = eine Million fünfhunderttausendzweiundsechzig
1.000.000.015 = eine Milliarde fünfzehn

Exercises

Which of these numbers are spelled out correcty?

1. a) einhundertvier   b) zweihundertzweizig
    c) dreihundertzehn   d) vierhundertervierzig

2. a) hundertsechzehn   b) hundertszehn
    c) einhundertszehn   d) einhundertzehn

3. a) tausendzwei   b) tausendzweihundertzweiundzweizig
    c) tausendzwanzig   d) tausendzweiundzwanzig

What is a million called in German?

4. a) eine Million   b) eine Milliarde

What is a billion called in German?

5. a) eine Billion   b) eine Milliarde

Chapter 3.4
Fractions and Percentages

We already touched on the terms for fractions in the chapter on reading the clock, where you learned that "ein Viertel" means a quarter. This provides a hint as to how fractions are constructed in general:

1/9 = ein Neuntel	1/8 = ein Achtel	1/7 = ein Siebtel
...	1/3 = ein Drittel	1/2 = einhalb

If you want to add a fraction to a regular number, this is how you express it:

3 1/3 = drei ein Drittel   4 2/8 = vier zwei Achtel
but: 5 1/2 = fünfeinhalb   2 1/2 = zweieinhalb etc.

Note that the capitalization of these fraction terms changes depending on whether they're used as a noun or an adjective:

Zwei **Drittel** des Landes bestehen aus Regenwald.
Two thirds of the country consists of rainforest.

Ich trank einen **drittel** Liter Orangensaft.
I drank a third of a liter of orange juice.

The noun version of "einhalb" is "die / eine Hälfte" and it is spelled out separately when used as an adjective:

Die **Hälfte** der Zeit ist vorbei.
One half of the time is over.

Der **halbe** Weg ist bereits geschafft.
We're already halfway there.

Eine **halbe** Stunde später waren wir fertig.
Half an hour later, we were done.

The German term for percent is "Prozent" and statements on percentages are constructed in a similar way to the English method:

The economy grew by 2.3 percent.
Die Wirtschaft wuchs um **2,3 Prozent**.

Notice that German employs a comma rather than a period to separate decimal places; this isn't just true for percentages, but in general.

If you want to describe a percentage of something, the German phrase to use is "Prozent von" or "Prozent der/des," depending on whether you're referencing something or someone that has a unique name (von) or a general noun (der/des):

30 percent of Europe consists of mountains
30 **Prozent von** Europa besteht aus Bergen.

15 percent of the economy consists of agriculture.
15 **Prozent der** Wirtschaft besteht aus Ackerbau.

If you want to express a percentage point change in something (e.g. your company's market share grew by 5 points from 20 to 25 percent), the German term to use is "Prozentpunkte":

Our company's market share grew by 5 percentage points.
Der Marktanteil unserer Firma ist um **5 Prozentpunkte** gestiegen.

Exercises

Find the wrongly spelled fraction terms

1. a) ein Fünftel   b) ein Dreitel
    c) ein Neuntel   d) ein Neuntes

2. a) eine Halbes   b) einhalb
    c) einehalbe   d) Halbe

3. a) zwei zwei Zweitel   b) zwei zwei Neuntel
    c) fünf und eine Halbe d) dreieinhalb

4. a) ein Hälftel   b) die Hälfte
    c) einhälftig   d) das Hälfte

Is the percentage term in this sentence used correctly?

5. 40 Prozent des Amerika lebt rural.
    a) yes   b) no

Chapter 4.1
Correct Usage of the Conjunctive Mood

By now, you've mastered the conjugation of German verbs in their basic form and can express things in the present, past, and future. But you also need the ability to express wishes, desires, and speculation, which is what the conjunctive mood (also called subjunctive mood) is for. In this subchapter, you'll learn how to construct it in German.

In case you're still completely confused as to what this mood is for, this would be an example of conjunctive mood usage in English:

If I was rich, I would move to California.

In German, this usage of the conjunctive mood is called "Konjunktiv II" and we will explore it more after delving into "Konjunktiv I." Konjunktiv I is mainly used to relay speech and to express in indirect quotations that you're reporting someone else's statements rather than making your own:

Peter says he is quite the craftsman.
Peter sagt, er **sei** ein toller Handwerker.

The essay deals with the question of whether the character is bad.
Der Aufsatz beschäftigt sich mit der Frage, ob der Charakter schlecht **sei**.

The Konjunktiv I conjugation for most verbs is regular, but "sein" is a rare exception. Note the difference between regular Konjunktiv I conjugation of "machen" and that of "sein":

ich	sei	mache
du	seiest	machest
er/sie/es	sei	mache
wir	seien	machen
ihr	seiet	machet
sie	seien	machen

You'll have to memorize the exceptions and apply them when appropriate.

Now let's explore the Konjunktiv II. As we already established above, it's used to express hypothetical scenarios or desires.

The inflection of the Konjunktiv II is based on whether the verb in question is a so-called strong verb or weak verb. Strong verbs typically have irregular conjugations in general and are characterized by a vowel shift in their stem vowel in the past sense. Weak verbs are usually regular verbs with regular past tense conjugations. The verbs "fahren" and "braten" which you learned in Chapter 2.4 are examples of strong verbs; "machen" would be a weak verb.

This is how the conjunction of these two groups vary in practice:

ich	führe	machte
du	führst	machtest
er/sie/es	führe	machte
wir	führen	machten
ihr	führt	machtet
sie	führen	machten

As you can see, the Konjunktiv II forms of "machen" are identical to its past tense whereas "fahren" has its own set of conjugation for this mood. Once again, there's no way but to memorize all the exceptions in order to reliably build correct Konjunktiv II forms.

Because the Konjunktiv II is identical to the past tense in weak verbs, they're typically assisted by the Konjunktiv version of "werden" which you familiarized with in Chapter 2.1:

ich	würde machen
du	würdest machen
er/sie/es	würde machen
wir	würden machen
ihr	würdet machen
sie	würden machen

Now let's apply this knowledge in some example sentences:

If I wasn't worrying so much, I would drive my car more often.
Wenn ich mir nicht so viele Gedanken **machen würde**, **führe** ich mein Auto öfter.

If I was younger, I would make different career choices.
Wenn ich jünger **wäre**, **würde** ich andere Karriere-Entscheidungen **machen**.

As you can see, "sein" also has irregular Konjunktiv II inflections:

ich	wäre
du	wärst
er/sie/es	wäre
wir	wären
ihr	wärt / wäret
sie	wären

Proficiency with the subjunctive mood adds to your ability to express nuance in German, so it's worth remembering the irregularities and exceptions!

Exercises

Which of these Konjunktiv I and II forms are correct?

1. a) seien   b) seier
   c) sein   d) wäre

2. a) wäret   b) seit
   c) seiet   d) wärtet

3. a) sei   b) sein
   c) wären   d) wärten

4. a) wäre   b) wärte
   c) seier   d) seitet

Are the Konjunktiv II forms used correctly in this sentence?

5. "Wenn ich mehr Auto **fahren würde, machte** mir das nichts aus."
   a) yes   b) no

Chapter 4.2
Constructing Compound Words

German is famous for its ability to form really long words. The stereotypical example that's often presented to language learners is "Donaudampfschiffkapitän," which translates to "captain of a Danube steam boat." After this subchapter, you too will have the means to construct barely pronounceable mega words!

The first thing to understand about German compound words is that the primary word that defines the meaning of the compound word must come last. In our example above, that would be "Kapitän" (captain): the word is ultimately about a captain and the rest of the word is just a closer description of his circumstances.

Apfelbaum**plantage** = a plantation containing apple trees
Ganzkörper**massage** = a massage of the whole body

The last word of the composite also determines the grammatical gender of the compound word and it's also the only part of the word subject to inflection:

Er besitzt einig**e** Apfelbaumplantage**n**.
He owns several apple tree plantations.

As you can already glean from the example term "Ganzkörpermassage," you can't just join nouns in German, but nouns and adjectives ("ganz") or nouns and verbs:

Löschwasser = water to extinguish (löschen) fire = fire extinguisher water
Aufräumarbeiten = work done to clear an area of debris or clutter (aufräumen)

Notice that the verbs lose their "en" ending for the purposes of adding them to a composite. There are various ways to smooth out words for the purpose of compounding them:

- Adding a vowel; Hund (dog) + Hütte (shed) = Hund**e**hütte
- Adding an s; Arbeit (job) + Amt (bureau) = Arbeit**s**amt (job center)
- Adding the plural form; Bild (picture) + Rahmen (frame) = Bild**er**rahmen

These smoothing operations don't necessarily follow a systematic set of rules and can also vary by region. However, through exposure and linguistic immersion, you'll eventually figure out what works in your area.

As fun as compound words can be, it's recommended to hyphenate the really long ones to improve the reading experience:

Maschine (machine) Produktion (production) Firma (company)
= Maschinenproduktionsfirma
= Maschinen-Produktionsfirma

But keep in mind that you may only use a hyphen in spots that haven't been smoothed out by an S. "Maschinenproduktions-Firma" would be grammatically incorrect.

Exercises

Going purely by sound and look, which of these compound words feel correctly constructed to you?

1. a) Hundfutter   b) Maschinenbau
   c) arbeitlos   d) Schiffenkapitän

2. a) Maschinenshütte b) Schiffenmaschine
   c) Schiffshund   d) Arbeitshund

3. a) Kapitänerhütte   b) Maschinenarbeit
   c) Kapitänsarbeit   d) Hundekapitän

4. a) Bau-Maschine   b) Baus-Maschinen
   c) Bauen-Maschine   d) Baumaschine

5. a) Hundes-Hütte   b) Hundehütte
   c) Hunde-Hütte   d) Hunden-Hütte

Chapter 4.3
Nuances of Prepositions

In any language, prepositions are small and frequently used terms that connect nouns to the larger portion of a sentence. As such, they are often required for conveying the meaning you want to convey. For instance, the phrase "I am waiting train station" could mean a lot of different things if we didn't have prepositions like "at," "over," "under," or "behind" to specify.

What's slightly difficult about German prepositions is their interaction with the case system. Some prepositions are followed by an accusative case, others by a dative case. You'll have to remember which prepositions belong to which group.

Accusative prepositions

"bis" (until, to, up to)

Du hast **bis** Montag Zeit.
You have time until Monday.

Ich gehe **bis** zum Ende der Stadt.
I walk to the end of town.

Der Aufzug trägt **bis** zu 500kg.
The elevator can carry up to 500kg.

"durch" (through)

Ich laufe **durch** die Stadt.
I walk through town.

"entlang" (along)

Ich fahre die Straße **entlang**.
I drive along the road.
(notice that this preposition is irregular and typically appears after the noun)

"für" (for)

Das ist **für** dich.
This is for you.

"gegen" (against)

Er kämpft **gegen** das Verbrechen.
He is fighting against crime.

"ohne" (without)

Ohne Kaffee kann ich nicht leben.
I can't live without coffee.

"um" (around, at)

Besuchen Sie mich **um** 1 Uhr.
Visit me at 1 o'clock.

Um den Marktplatz versammelten sich die Menschen.
The people gathered around the market square.

Dative prepositions

"aus" (from, out of)

Er kam **aus** dem Flughafen.
He came out of the airport.

Er kommt **aus** Deutschland.
He is from Germany.

"bei" (at, near)

Wir treffen uns heute **bei** Peter.
Today we meet at Peter's.

Das Haus liegt **bei** der alten Fabrik.
The house is located near the old factory.

"mit" (with)

Ich treffe mich heute **mit** Peter.
I am meeting with Peter today.

"nach" (after, to)

Es ist **nach** 8 Uhr.
It is after 8 o'clock.

Ich ziehe **nach** Deutschland.
I am moving to Germany.

"seit" (since)

Wir sind **seit** 1990 verheiratet.
We have been married since 1990.

"von" (from, of)

Ich komme **von** einem anderen Planeten.
I come from another planet.

Ich bin Teil **von** ihrer Gruppe.
I am a part of her group.

"zu" (to)

Lass uns zu Peter gehen.
Let us go to Peter.

Lastly, there's a group of prepositions that can use both cases depending on whether you're referring to a movement to another place (accusative) or describe a currently existing location (dative).

These prepositions include:

"an / am" (on, to)

"Ich gehe **an** den Bahnhof" versus "Ich bin **am** Bahnhof"
"I go to the train station" (accusative) versus "I am at the train station" (dative)

"auf" (on, upon)

"Ich gehe **auf** die Schule" versus "Ich gehe **auf** der Straße"
"I go to school" (accusative) versus "I walk on the street" (dative)

"in" (in, into)

"Ich gehe **in** die Bar" versus "Ich bin **in** der Bar"
"I go to the bar" (accusative) versus "I am at the bar" (dative)

Exercises

Which of these prepositions are accusative prepositions?

1. a) mit   b) aus
   c) ohne   d) um

2. a) seit   b) zu
    c) gegen   d) durch

3. a) auf   b) bei
    c) nach   d) in

In German, which cases would apply to the objects in these sentences?

4. "I stand on the roof"
    a) accusative   b) dative

5. "I go on vacation"
    a) accusative   b) dative

Chapter 4.4
Comma Placement

The correct usage of punctuation marks is very important to convey meaning in any language. Fortunately, the rules governing comma placement in German are very consistent and rather quick to pick up.

The first and most important function of commas in German is to separate main and subordinate clauses. Unlike in the English language, a comma must always separate these two.

Ich gehe in ein Restaurant, **weil** ich hungrig bin
I go to a restaurant because I am hungry.

Weil ich hungrig bin, gehe ich in ein Restaurant.
Because I am hungry, I go to a restaurant.

Two consecutive main clauses can also always be separated by a comma, but need not necessarily be separated by a comma if they are joined by the words "und" (and) or "or" (oder).

Ich gehe heute in ein Restaurant **und** morgen gehe ich ins Kino.
Today I go to a restaurant and tomorrow I go to the cinema.

Ich gehe heute in ein Restaurant, **oder** vielleicht gehe ich auch ins Kino.
Today I go to a restaurant or maybe I go to the cinema.

Commas are used to create enumerations and lists in exactly the same way they are in English:

Ich gehe heute ins Kino, ins Restaurant und in den Supermarkt.
Today I go to the cinema, the restaurant **and** the grocery store.

They are also used to demarcate appositives in the same way:

Das Restaurant, ein wirklich vornehmes Lokal, beeindruckte meine Freunde.
The restaurant, a really fancy place, impressed my friends.

When it comes to direct speech, the rules are slightly different. Direct speech in English can be initiated with a comma or a colon, but always requires a colon in German:

Er sagte: "Lass uns in ein Restaurant gehen."
He said, "Let's go to a restaurant."

If the direct speech part of the sentence precedes the main clause, the comma separating the two sentence parts must be outside, not inside the quotation marks:

"Lass uns in ein Restaurant gehen", sagte er.
"Let's go to a restaurant," he said.

Lastly, when directly addressing people, a comma should be put after the greeting phrase just like in English:

Mein Sohn, ich grüße dich.
My son, I greet you.

Exercises

Which of the following sentences contain correct punctuation?

1. a) Ich gehe in ein Restaurant, oder Café.
   b) Ich gehe in ein Restaurant oder Café.
   c) Ich gehe, in ein Restaurant oder Café.
   d) Ich gehe, in Restaurant, oder Café.

2. a) Weil ich hungrig bin gehe ich ins Café.
   b) Ich gehe ins Café, weil ich hungrig bin.
   c) Ich gehe ins Café weil ich hungrig bin.
   d) Weil ich hungrig bin, gehe ich ins Café.

3. a) Ich gehe ins Café, ins Restaurant und ins Kino.
   b) Ich gehe ins Café ins Restaurant und ins Kino.
   c) Ich gehe, ins Café, ins Restaurant und ins Kino.
   d) Ich gehe ins Café, ins Restaurant oder ins Kino.

Are the following statements true or not?

4. All subordinate clauses in German are separated by a comma.
   a) Yes   b) No

5. Punctuation in direct speech works the same in German as in English.
   a) Yes   b) No

Chapter 4.5
Subordinate clauses

Subordinate clauses are dependent clauses that are meant to give additional context or descriptive elements to a main clause. They cannot stand on their own since they require a main clause to refer to. You already learned in the previous chapter that they are always separated by a comma. In this chapter you will learn about the different types of subordinate clauses that exist in German and the specific conjunctions required to construct them.

Conditional clauses

These clauses are meant to convey that something will only happen if a certain condition is met. The relevant conjunctions are "wenn" or "falls" (if) and "sobald" (when).

Wenn/Falls du in den Zoo gehst, besuche die Löwen.
If you go to the zoo, do visit the lions.
Ich werde die Löwen besuchen, **sobald** ich die Elefanten besucht habe.
I will visit the lions when I have visited the elephants.

Relative clauses

Relative clauses add additional information to a noun and are constructed with the relative pronouns you have already encountered in chapter 1.4.

Der Zoo, **der** wirklich fantastisch ist, beherbergt viele Löwen.
The zoo, which is really fantastic, hosts many lions.

Ich besuche im Zoo gern die Löwen, **die** sehr imposant sind.
I like to visit the lions, which are very impressive, at the zoo.

Causal clauses

Whenever a causal explanation for something is required, we use subordinate causal clauses to illustrate that. Their German conjunctions are "da", "weil" and "denn" (because, since, as).

Da die Löwen immer hungrig sind, braucht der Zoo viel Fleisch.
Since the lions are always hungry, the zoo needs lots of meat.

Die Löwen werden am Abend müde, **weil** sie am Tag so viel spielen.
The lions get tired in the evenings as they play so much during the day.

Kinder mögen Löwen gern, **denn** sie sehen sehr abenteuerlich aus.
Children like lions because they look so adventurous.

Purpose clauses

If an action has an expected or desired consequence or reason, a purpose clause can be employed to explain that relationship. German knows the conjunctions "dass" (that), "damit" (so that) and "um zu" (in order to, so as to).

Es ist wahr, **dass** die Löwen manchmal sehr laut sind.
It is true that the lions are sometimes very loud.

Ich werde mich beeilen, **damit** ich noch am Morgen in den Zoo komme.
I will hurry so that I can enter the zoo during the morning.

Um mit Löwen **zu** spielen, muss man mutig sein.
In order to play with lions, one must be bold.

Concessive clauses

Those are used to express a contradiction or contrast. The conjunction you need to learn here is "obwohl" (although, even though).

Ich will die Löwen besuchen, **obwohl** das Wetter schlecht ist.
I want to visit the lions even though the weather is poor.

Obwohl ich oft ängstlich bin, mag ich die Löwen.
Although I'm often frightful, I like the lions.

Exercises

You have previously learned about a related, but different group of words called prepositions. Find the conjunctions in this sea of conjunctions and prepositions.

1. a) durch   b) damit   c) denn   d) doch
2. a) um zu   b) um   c) ohne   d) obwohl
3. a) auf   b) ab   c) wenn   d) von

Which of these conjunctions are causal conjunctions?

4. a) weil   b) dass   c) damit   d) denn

Which of these conjunctions are conditional conjunctions?

5. a) da   b) wenn   c) falls   d) sobald

Chapter 4.6
Nonfinite verb forms

Y ou have learned in previous chapters how to conjugate verbs, but sometimes it is necessary to use special verb forms to form specific sentence structures or express certain meanings. This chapter will teach you about the times when this is necessary and the basics of how to create these verb forms since there are, as you may have expected, some more irregularities involved.

Infinitive forms

In previous chapters you have already learned the basic, infinitive forms of a number of verbs such as "fahren" or "sein". Typically verbs have to be conjugated to express person, mood or tense in order to make any sense, but there are occasions for the infinitive form too:

- When they follow a modal verb, as you already discovered in chapter 2.3

  Wir müssen nach Hause **fahren**.
  We must drive home.

- When used in an infinitive clause to express an intention or purpose. In these cases, the infinitive form is accompanied by the word "zu":

  Ich habe keine Lust, meine Hausaufgaben **zu machen**.
  I don't have motivation to do my homework.

Gerunds

A gerund is a modified verb that complements its original verb-like qualities (describing an action or a state of mind or feeling) with those of a noun (describing a thing or an idea). In German, gerunds are formed as nominalized verbs in the infinitive form and are preceded by the (sometimes inflected) neutral relative pronoun "das".

I mag **(das) Tanzen** viel mehr als meine Hausaufgaben zu machen.
I enjoy dancing much more than doing my homework.

Ich widmete mich **dem Lösen** der Aufgabe.
I devoted myself to solving the task.

Participles

There are two kinds of participle forms in German called Partizip I and Partizip II. Partizip I refers to a simultaneous action in the present and is also used to construct progressive tenses in German. It is formed by adding a –d to the infinitive form of a verb, for example "fahren" turns into "fahrend". It is inflected the same way as an adjective when used in combination with a noun.

Auto **fahrend** hörte ich Musik.

I listened to music while driving a/the car.

Das schnell **fahrende** Auto erschreckte mich.
The rapidly driving car startled me.

Partizip II is the more difficult of the two as it is formed more irregularly. It is both the basis for building the perfect tense which you have not yet encountered in this language guide, but can also be used in adjective form to describe things that happened in the past and are still having an effect now. They are then inflected as any adjective would be.

In regular verbs, it it constructed by adding a –ge to the infinitive form of the verb. For instance, the Partizip II of "fahren" is "gefahren". Irregular verbs can come in many shapes and sizes and you will have to once again memorize the exceptions. Some examples:

sein (be) -> **gewesen**
hören (hear) -> **ge**hör**t**
gehen (walk) -> **gegangen**

To make matters worse, these Partizip II forms in their perfect tense also use two different modal verbs, "sein" and "haben", and there is no particular pattern to their usage either. We still find some echoes of this in old English, where sentences like "I am become king" provide evidence of the usage of "be" instead of "have" as the modal verb in a perfect tense construction, but in today's regular English this rarely exists anymore. In contrast, German:

ich bin gefahren
ich habe gehört
ich bin gegangen
ich bin gewesen

Ich **bin** in den Zoo **gegangen**.
I have gone to the zoo.

Im Zoo fand ich eine **gefüllte** Wasserflasche.
I found a filled water bottle at the zoo.

Exercises

Which infinitive forms have been constructed correctly?

1. a) Ich muss meine Hausaufgaben zu machen.
    b) Ich will meine Hausaufgaben nicht zu machen.
    c) Ich werde meine Hausaufgaben machen.
    d) Hausaufgaben zu machen ist schön.

2. a) Ich habe nach Hause fahren keine Lust.
   b) Ich habe keine Lust, nach Hause zu fahren.
   c) Ich will nach Hause fahren.
   d) Heute darf ich nach Hause zu fahren.

Which of the following statements about gerunds are true?

3. Gerunds are formed as full verbs in German
   a) yes   b) no

4. Gerunds cannot be inflected in German.
   a) yes   b) no

Which of these Partizip I and II forms are potentially correct?

5. a) fahrende   b) gefahrend
   c) gefahren   d) fahrenden

Chapter 4.7
Passive voice

As a last lesson in your advanced grammar curriculum, you will learn how to build the passive voice in German. Some information from the previously chapter will come in handy here.

The passive voice form of a verb indicates that the subject of the sentence *is being done something to* rather than *doing something*. In English, it is constructed with the modal verb "be" and the perfect verb tense, for example "I was punished". In German, the auxiliary verb "werden" is used in conjunction with the Partizip II. Let us quickly review the present and past tense forms of "werden":

ich	werde, wurde
du	wirst, wurdest
er, sie, es	wird, wurde
wir	werden, wurden
ihr	werdet, wurdet
sie	werden, wurden

Some example sentences:

Ich **werde** nach Hause **gefahren**.
I am being driven home.

Wir **wurden** von unserem Freund **besucht**.
We were visited by our friend.

As is the case with modal verb constructions in German generally, the auxiliary verb takes the typical place of the verb in the sentence structure and the actual verb is placed at the end of the sentence.

When adding an object to the sentence, the equivalent term to the English "by" is "von":

Wir **wurden von** unserem Freund nach Hause **gefahren**.
We were driven home by our friend.

If you want to use a passive voice construction for the future tense, indicating that someone or someone will be done something to in the future, you have to use the simple future tense of "werden", which is "werden werden":

Wir **werden** von unserem Freund nach Hause **gefahren werden**.
We will be driven home by our friend.

You will notice how in this particular case, the infinitive form of the auxiliary verb takes the last spot in the sentence rather than the actual verb.

In colloquial language, usage of the passive voice is less common since it is considered a bit of a sophisticated verb form best reserved for formal writing or speaking. Typically people prefer to speak in the active tense:

Unser Freund **wird** uns nach Hause **fahren**.
Our friend will drive us home.

Exercises

Identify the correctly constructed passive voice forms:

1. a) Ich werde in den Zoo fahren.
    b) Ich werde in den Zoo fahrend.
    c) Ich werde in den Zoo gefahren.
    d) Ich werde in den Zoo gefahren werden.

2. a) Du wurdest von deinem Freund in den Zoo gefahren.
    b) Du wurdest gefahren von deinem Freund in den Zoo.
    c) Du wurdest gefahren werden in den Zoo.
    d) Du wurdest in den Zoo gefahren werden.

3. a) Wir werden in den Zoo gefahren werden.
    b) Wir werden werden in den Zoo gefahren.
    c) Wir werden in den Zoo gefahren.
    d) Wir werden in den Zoo fahrend.

Which of the following statements about the passive voice is correct?

4. The passive voice can be formed with multiple auxiliary verbs.
    a) yes   b) no

5. The passive voice is more of a formal phenomenon in German.
    a) yes   b) no

Chapter 5.1
"False friend" terms
for English speakers

After all this grammatical exercise, it is time for you to learn some words, and you will start your journey by learning about the most deceptive ones: so-called false friends that are spelled similarly in English, but mean very different things in German.

aktuell – actual

Whereas "actual" describes something existing in reality, "aktuell" means current or up to date.

Die aktuelle Mode ist wunderschön.
The current fashion is beautiful.

also – also

The English "also" means "in addition to something" while the German "also" is akin to "so" or "therefore".

Wir gehen also in den Zoo.
Therefore we go to the zoo.

Art – art

While the English "art" describes a form of creative expression, the German noun "Art" means "type" or "kind".

Ein Zoo ist eine Art Freizeitbeschäftigung.
A zoo is a type of leisure activity.

bald – bald

The English adjective "bald" describes a loss of hair while the German "bald" means "soon".

Wir werden bald in den Zoo gehen.
Wir will soon go to the zoo.

bekommen – become

"Become" denotes a process of transformation or change, but "bekommen" in German means "receive" or simply "get".

Zu Weihnachten bekommen wir Geschenke.
We receive presents on Christmas.

Chef – chef

In English, a "chef" is a cook whereas in German, a "Chef" is a boss or supervisor.

Mein Chef hat mir eine Gehaltserhöhung gegeben.
My boss has given me a raise.

eventuell – eventually

"Eventually" in English means "at some point in the future" whereas in German it describes a general possibility or chance.

Eventuell gehen wir morgen in den Zoo.
Maybe we go to the zoo tomorrow.

Fabrik – fabric

A German Fabrik (factory) might produce things made out of fabric, but not necessarily!

Ich arbeite in einer Fabrik.
I work in a factory.

Gift – gift

A very dangerous false friend: the English "gift" means "present", but the German "Gift" means "poison"!

Von Gift sollte man sich stets fernhalten.
One should always stay away from poison.

Gymnasium – gymnasium

While the English gymnasium is a sports facility, the German Gymnasium is a secondary school that prepares students for a university education.

Ich war 9 Jahre lang auf dem Gymnasium.
I attended Gymnasium for 9 years.

Handy – handy

The English adjective "handy" means something is comfortable to have or handle, but the German noun "Handy" means cell phone.

Mein Handy war sehr teuer.
My call phone was very expensive.

Kostüm – custom

This can be a bit of a false friend in English, too. The German "Kostüm" is a disguise or special outfit, a bit like the English "costume", but not "custom" as in "made according to someone's specification".

Ich gehe in einem Kostüm auf die Halloween-Party.
I attend the Halloween party in a costume.

Mist – mist

The English "mist" is another word for "fog"; in contrast, the German "Mist" means "dung" or "manure"!

Der Bauer streute den Mist auf seine Felder.
The farmer distributed the manure on his fields.

Rat – rat

In English, rats are furry little rodents, but the German version of the noun describes "advice" or "hint". It can also describe a councilperson in certain jurisdictions.

Sie hat mir guten Rat gegeben.
She gave me good advice.

Er ist ein Stadtrat.
He is a city councilor.

sensibel – sensible

This is a false friend that many Germans learning English initially struggle with: "sensible" means "practical" in English, but "sensibel" means "sensitive" in German!

Ich bin manchmal sehr sensibel.
I am very sensitive sometimes.

Exercises

Identify the correct meanings of the following false friend terms:

1. eventuell
   a) current   b) maybe   c) at some point   d) fancy

2. bekommen
   a) will be   b) possess   c) receive   d) withhold

3. Art
   a) kind   b) creativity   c) hope   d) change

4. Rat
   a) advice   b) neglect   c) councilperson   d) boss

5. also
   a) in addition   b) despite   c) but   d) therefore

Chapter 5.2
Hints for finding the right noun gender

Given that German has three separate grammatical genders and each noun belongs to one of them, it would be very helpful to have some rules to refer to when figuring out which noun might be which. Unfortunately, none of these rules are ironclad and there are typically some exceptions to each, but in general, they provide a good framework. And don't worry if you struggle: this is usually one of the aspects of the German language that people take the longest to get comfortable with.

Grammatical genders in German can be identified quite well based on the endings of nouns. This is what that looks like for the three different genders:

Masculine nouns

These nouns typically end on –en, -er, -ig, -ling, or –m.

en	der Boden (floor), der Süden (south), der Kuchen (cake)
er	der Spieler (player), der Richter (judge), der Träger (carrier)
ig	der König (king), der Teig (dough), der Essig (vinegar)
ling	der Schönling (beau), der Häuptling (chief), der Frühling (spring)
m	der Wurm (worm), der Oheim (uncle), der Arm (arm)

Feminine nouns

Common endings for those are –e, -ei, -heit, -keit, -schaft and –ung. However, the actual word "Ei" (egg) is neutral: "das Ei"!

e	die Schnecke (snail), die Reise (journey), die Hütte (hut)
ei	die Reederei (wharf), die Schwärmerei (infatuation), die Türkei (Turkey)
heit	die Einfachheit (simplicity), die Bosheit (spite), die Weisheit (wisdom)
keit	die Heiterkeit (hilarity), die Machbarkeit (feasibility), die Dankbarkeit (gratitude)
schaft	die Freundschaft (friendship), die Feindschaft (hostility), die Mannschaft (sports team)
ung	die Trauung (wedding), die Scheidung (divorce), die Rettung (rescue)

Neutral nouns

Lastly, that group of nouns often ends on –ment, -nis and –um.

ment	das Firmament (firmament), das Monument (monument), das Dokument (document)
nis	das Hindernis (obstacle), das Geheimnis (secret), das Ereignis (event)
um	das Fürstentum (principality), das Datum (date), das Drumherum (trappings)

Exercises

Based on the approximate rules you have just learned, identify the correctly gendered nouns:

1. a) der Fühler   b) der Frechheit   c) der Turm   d) der Hoheit
2. a) die Roggen   b) die Rohheit   c) die Widerling   d) die Gram
3. a) das Honig   b) das Herzogtum   c) das Leistung   d) das Album
4. a) der Norden   b) die Ereignis   c) das Ärgernis   d) die Übung
5. a) das Träumerei   b) das Westen   c) die Mongolei   d) der Osten

Chapter 5.3
Common words with multiple connotations

Like most languages, German contains a number of words that can have different meanings based on context and that might confuse a student of the language. In this chapter, we will go over some of them in order to help you navigate the pitfalls of double meanings!

Bank

The German noun "Bank" does in fact have three different meanings. The first meaning is one that English speakers are also familiar with: financial institutions.

Ich gehe zur **Bank**, um Geld zu holen.
I go to the bank to get cash.

Its second meaning is equivalent to the English "bench":

Im Park setzte ich mich auf eine **Bank**.
I sat down on a bench in the park.

Its third and last meaning, typically accompanied by the word "Fenster" (window), refers to windowsills:

Heute werde ich die Fenster**bank** reinigen.
Today I will clean the windowsill.

Gang

This word, too, has three different meanings; in fact, one could argue it has four nowadays if we count the English meaning of "gang" as in "organized criminal group" since it has also made its way into the German language.

But as for the three original meanings, one of them is "gear" in the context of an engine:

Mein Auto hat fünf **Gänge**.
My car has five gears.

A Gang could also be a type of hallway in a building:

Meine Wohnung liegt am Ende des **Ganges**.
My apartment is situated at the end of the hallway.

Lastly, "Gang" could refer to the way someone walks:

Sein **Gang** war gemütlich und beschwingt.
His walking style was cozy and cheery.

Sinn

This is yet another German word with three meanings. It first of all connotes that something makes sense:

Das ergibt **Sinn**!
This makes sense!

But then it could also refer to one of your five senses:

Mein Geruchs**sinn** ist leicht zu reizen.
My sense of smell is easily triggered.

Finally, one could use the term to express purpose or meaning:

Der **Sinn** der Aufgabe war mir unverständlich.
I did not understand the meaning of the task.

Schloss

Our last example for this chapter, and this time it only has two meanings! One of them is "castle":

Wir haben in unserem Urlaub ein **Schloss** besichtigt.
We have visited a castle on our vacation.

The secondary meaning is "lock":

Das **Schloss** an meiner Tür ist defekt.
My door's lock is broken.

Exercises

1. Which of those meanings does "Bank" have?
   a) stool   b) sill   c) bench   d) branch

2. Which of those meanings does "Gang" have?
   a) walk   b) cove   c) gear   d) lock

3. Which of those meanings does "Sinn" have?
   a) desire   b) luck   c) sense   d) purpose

4. Which of those meanings does "Schloss" have?
   a) plan   b) lock   c) attempt   d) castle

5. True or false: different connotations of the same word are accompanied by different grammatical genders.
   a) true   b) false

Chapter 5.4
Getting negation right

Typically, students of the German language struggle a bit with the difference between the German "nicht" (not) and "kein" ("no" as an adjective) since their usage appears a bit random. Let's illustrate that with a few example sentences:

She does not speak with him anymore.
Sie redet **nicht** mehr mit ihm.

She does not speak German.
Sie spricht **kein** Deutsch.

She does not speak German well.
She spricht **nicht** gut Deutsch.

She has no good words to say about him.
Sie hat **keine** guten Worte über ihn zu sagen.

But there actually are a few rules governing this:

1. If the English phrase contains an adjective "no", you can always use the "kein" translation:

   I have no interest in this.
   Ich habe daran **kein** Interesse.

2. If the object in the sentence is an accusative case object, then "not" is typically also translated as "kein", though you can often also use "nicht" if you slightly alter the sentence structure:

   She does not go to the supermarket.
   Sie geht **in keinen** Supermarkt.
   Sie geht **nicht in den** Supermarkt.

   This only works if there is a preposition involved, in this case "in". Thus, the sentence "I don't speak German" cannot be altered in such a way and you should always employ "kein".

3. If the object in the sentence is a dative case object, then "not" is always translated as "nicht":

   I do not agree with you.
   Ich stimme **nicht** mit dir überein.

Double negation works similar to the way it does in English as well:

Er ist **niemals nicht** beschäftigt.
He is never not busy.

Of course, like in English, it would be more elegant to simply use an affirmation rather than a double negation:

Er ist **immer** beschäftigt.
He is always busy.

Exercises

Which of the following sentences are negated correctly?

1. a) Sie redet keine mit ihm.
    b) Sie nicht redet mit ihm.
    c) Sie redet nicht mit ihm.
    d) Sie nicht mit ihm redet.

2. a) Er spricht keine Deutsch.
    b) Er nicht spricht Deutsch.
    c) Er spricht kein Deutsch.
    d) Er spricht Deutsch nicht.

3. a) Wir gehen nicht in den Zoo.
    b) Wir nicht gehen in den Zoo.
    c) Wir gehen in keine Zoo.
    d) Wir gehen in keinen Zoo.

Which of the following statements are true?

4. German allows for double negation in statements.
    a) true   b) false

5. The words "nicht" and "kein" are arbitrarily replaceable.
    a) true   b) false

Chapter 5.5
Tips for correct word ordering

You have already learned a bit about sentence structure and word ordering in previous chapters, but since this can be an overwhelming subject matter, our last subchapter in advanced grammar will give you some pointers to go by when trying to construct a sentence.

Let's revisit the very basics. German sentences follow the subject verb object structure (SVO):

Peter ging in den Zoo.
Peter went to the zoo.

It is possible to switch out the position of subject and object to put emphasis on the object:

In den Zoo ging Peter.
To the zoo went Peter.

But this is typically used in more lyrical contexts. What you will find used more frequently is a switcheroo of adverbs, for instance expressions of time and place:

Ich gehe **heute** in den Zoo.
I go to the zoo today.

Heute gehe ich in den Zoo.
Today I go to the zoo.

Again, this is meant to put emphasis on the adverb rather than the subject.

Speaking of adverbs, their placement deviates slightly from their English equivalents. In English, the order of placement is "manner, place, time" (MPT):

I **hastily** went to my **friend's house yesterday**.

In German, the ordering is "time, manner, place":

Ich ging **gestern hastig** zu meinem **Freund**.

And of course you can also switch those up to change the emphasis:

Zu meinem Freund ging ich gestern hastig.

Hastig ging ich gestern zu meinem Freund.

Gestern ging ich hastig zu meinem Freund.

One type of clause you haven't learned about yet is the **imperative clause**. It is the kind of clause used when exhorting or admonishing someone to do something:

Open the door, please!

Unlike in English, the German imperative has its own conjugation; for most words, it is the regular first person singular inflection of the verb when addressing someone in the second person singular, informal way, **or** the infinitive form when addressing them with the more respectful "Sie". Notice how the personal pronoun only pops up in the respectful variant of the imperative:

Öffne die Tür, bitte!
Öffnen Sie die Tür, bitte!

Also notice how the verb, much like in interrogative clauses, comes **first**, unlike in typical main clauses where it comes **second**.

One of the few exceptions in the imperative conjugation is "sein" (be), where the Konjunktiv I forms you learned about previously are being employed:

Sei gesegnet!
Seien Sie gesegnet!
Be blessed!

Exercises

Which of the following statements are true?

1. All words in German sentences can be switched around at will.
   a) true   b) false

2. All adverbs in German sentences can trade positions at will.
   a) true   b) false

3. The typical succession of adverbs is the same in German as in English.
   a) true   b) false

Which of these clauses have the correct word ordering?

4. a) Die Tür Sie können öffnen?
   b) Können Sie die Tür öffnen?
   c) Die Tür Sie öffnen!
   d) Öffnen Sie die Tür!

5. a) Peter die Tür öffnet.
   b) Peter hastig die Tür öffnet.
   c) Peter öffnet hastig die Tür.
   d) Die Tür öffnet Peter hastig.

Chapter 6.1
Job interviews

Now that your head is filled with grammar, verbs and at least some words, it's time to graduate to whole phrases that might be useful in a given context. The first installation of this series will deal with job interviews. The following subchapters will be structured to give you an idea of a situation where a phrase might come in handy, then list the phrase, and then explain the details of the phrase.

Let's imagine you applied for a job and got a positive response. Now you have arrived at your employer's location and need to find your interview partner, Mr. Müller. You enter the building and spot a receptionist, whom you approach.

"Guten Tag. Können Sie mir helfen? Ich suche Herrn Müller."
"Good day. Can you help me? I'm looking for Mr. Müller."

Don't forget to say "Vielen Dank!" after you received your information.

Now you are waiting in front of Mr. Müller's office; eventually he invites you in. You shake hands and exchange pleasantries:

"Guten Tag, Herr Müller. Es freut mich sehr, Sie kennenzulernen!"
"Good day, Mr. Müller. I am very happy to make your acquaintance!"

After Mr. Müller asks you some question about your professional history and skills, he might eventually pass the conversation over to you and ask if you have any questions. Here are some good ones you might want to ask:

"Welche Möglichkeiten zur beruflichen Entwicklung bietet Ihr Unternehmen?"
"Which possibilities for career advancement does your company offer?"

"Können Sie mir den typischen Ablauf in einem Ihrer Projekte beschreiben?"
"Can you give me an overview of how your team might approach a project?"

"Wie würden Sie Ihre Unternehmenskultur beschreiben?"
"How would you describe your company culture?"

These questions show interest in the details of the business on your part and will hopefully score points with any HR professional.

After you conclude the interview, some nice finishing phrases would be:

"Vielen Dank für das Gespräch. Ich hoffe, ich konnte Sie überzeugen!"
"Thanks a lot for the interview. I hope I could convince you!"

"Wenn Sie noch Fragen haben, können Sie mich jederzeit anrufen oder mir eine Mail schreiben."
"If you have further questions, you can call or e-mail me any time."

And that will hopefully get you the job!

Exercises

Which of the following statements are true?

1. Pleasantries such as "please" and "thank you" are not as important in German.
    a) true   b) false

2. You should ask if someone may help you before you make a request.
    a) true   b) false

3. During a job interview in Germany, you can expect to mostly get asked questions, not the other way around.
    a) true   b) false

4. It's a good idea to inquire about the Unternehmenskultur.
    a) true   b) false

5. You should reassure your interview partner in a job interview that you are always available for clarification.
    a) true   b) false

Chapter 6.2
Judicial system

Of course we all hope you won't have any involuntary dealings with the judicial system in Germany, but especially as an ex-pat, you might have to deal with some aspects of it to get your visa renewed, initiate a naturalization process or maybe work out details regarding a marriage. So here are some useful phrases to employ when dealing with the German judicial system.

Let's start with some words that might come up. A court in German is called "ein Gericht". Incidentally, this word also has a double meaning as "food dish". Unless you plan to pursue intricate legal cases, chances are you will mostly be interacting with the local equivalent of a magistrates' court, which is called "Amtsgericht". The Cologne magistrates' court, for instance, would be "Amtsgericht Köln".

For most administrative matters, you might not need a lawyer, but if you do, you will be looking for "ein Anwalt" or "ein Rechtsanwalt". The state prosecutor is called "ein Staatsanwalt" and a judge would be "ein Richter".

Now let's assume you just want to extend your visa. Since many administrative processes of this nature still have to be managed in person in current Germany, you might have to show up at the local magistrates' court and go to, say, room 105. There, you can employ the charms you already practiced with the receptionist in the previous subchapter:

"Guten Tag. Können Sie mir helfen? Ich suche Raum 105."
"Good day. Can you help me? I'm looking for room 105."

After you find room 105, you want to ask the clerk for a visa extension and maybe some related questions.

"Guten Tag. Ich möchte gern mein Visum verlängern."
"Good day. I would like to extend my visa."

"Welche Dokumente werden dafür benötigt?"
"Which documents are needed for that?"

"Wie lange wird dieser Prozess benötigen?"
"How long will this process take?"

"Wie viel wird dieser Vorgang kosten?"
"How much will this procedure cost?"

"Welche dieser Dinge kann ich auch online erledigen?"
"Which of these things can I do online as well?"

Of course these phrases will also be useful when asking about the details of any kind of official business.

If you find yourself in the situation where you have to file a legal complaint or report, you will be interacting with police rather than the courts. That conversation might go as follows:

"Guten Tag. Ich möchte gern eine Anzeige erstatten."
"Good day. I would like to file a legal report."

"Ich möchte einen Diebstahl anzeigen."
"Ich would like to report a theft."

"Ich möchte einen Verkehrsunfall melden."
"I would like to report a traffic accident."

"Ich möchte eine Vermisstenanzeige aufgeben."
"I would like to report a missing person."

And if you ever find yourself in a courtroom, don't forget to use the German equivalent for the honorific "Your Honor": "Euer Ehren".

Exercises

1. A judge in German is called …
    a) Anwalt　　　b) Staatsanwalt　　　c) Richter　　d) Gericht

2. When you report something to the police, you file a …
    a) Anklage　　　b) Anzeige　　　c) Anwalt　　d) Vorgang

3. Very few procedural tasks have to be done in person in Germany.
    a) True　　　b) False

4. In Germany, your legal issues will most likely be solved by a …
    a) Staatsanwalt　b) Amtsgericht　　c) Polizei　　d) Prozess

5. German judges are to be addressed by "Euer Ehren".
    a) True　　　b) False

Chapter 6.3
Party conversation and meeting new people

Now let's graduate to something more casual and less official. Imagine you're at a party in the evening trying to meet new people and start a conversation. There's of course the classic evergreen method:

"Hallo, wie geht es dir?"
"Hey, how are you?"

If you find yourself in more serious and less casual company, it's always good to use the respectful pronoun "Sie":

"Hallo, wie geht es Ihnen?"

Keep this in mind for all the example phrases you will learn here.

You could also inquire about people's names:

"Hallo, wie heißt du?"
"Hey, what is your name?"

And then, depending on where the conversation goes, you could ask a number of things:

"Wie gefällt dir die Party?"
"How do you like the party?"

"Was machst du so beruflich?"
"And what do you professionally?"

"Was studierst du?"
"What subject are you majoring in?"

"Gefällt dir die Musik hier?"
"Do you like the music here?"

"Machst du gern Sport?"
"Do you play any sports?"

If you hit it off with your new friend and want to maintain contact, there are a few phrases you could bring up:

"Hast du Lust, dass wir uns nächste Woche wieder treffen?"
"Would you like to meet again next week?"

"Darf ich deine Handynummer wissen?"
"May I learn your cell phone number?"

"Was hast du nächstes Wochenende vor?"
"What plans do you have for next weekend?"

Finally, you want to say goodbye in a nice and charming way:

"War total nett, mit dir zu reden. Hoffentlich bis bald!"
"Was totally nice to talk to you. Until soon, hopefully!"

"Vielleicht sehen wir uns später noch einmal. Mach's gut!"
"Maybe we'll run into each other again later. See you!"

Exercises

1. Which of these are grammatically correct greeting phrases?
   a) Wie geht es dir?
   b) Geht es?
   c) Ihnen geht es?
   d) Wie geht es Ihnen?

Identify the correct party phrases:

2. a) Vielen Dank für das Gespräch.
   b) Ich möchte eine Anzeige erstatten.
   c) Machst du gern Sport?
   d) Was studierst du?

3. a) Wie heißen Sie?
   b) Was machen Sie beruflich?
   c) Welche Möglichkeiten der beruflichen Entwicklung bieten Sie?
   d) Machst du gern Sport?

4. Finish the sentence. "Darf ich deine Handynummer ..."
   a) sehen   b) hören   c) wissen   d) lernen

5. Finish the sentence. "Was hast du nächstes Wochenende ..."
   a) auf   b) in   c) zu   d) vor

Chapter 6.4
Resolving verbal conflicts

As much as we would like to avoid getting dragged into fights, sometimes it just happens and we need some diplomatic phrases to calm the situation down. You will learn some of them in this subchapter.

Let's assume you are confused by the sudden emergence of this conflict and want to know what the issue even is:

"Entschuldigen Sie bitte, was genau ist das Problem?"
"Please excuse me, what exactly is the problem?"

If you fail to understand the explanation, you can ask for clarification:

"Können Sie mir das bitte noch einmal langsamer erklären?"
"Can you please explain this to me again and more slowly?"

After you have ascertained the nature of the problem, you now want to cool the situation down:

"Bitte entschuldigen Sie, wenn ich Sie verärgert habe."
"Please excuse me if I offended you."

"Wir können hier bestimmt eine gute Lösung finden."
"I'm sure we can find a good solution here."

"Wie würden Sie die Situation gern lösen?"
"How would you like to solve the situation?"

Now you can hear the other person out and figure out where they are coming from and what they might want to see changed. Maybe that is not entirely to your liking though and you need to find a compromise solution:

"Ich verstehe Ihren Ärger und das war nicht meine Absicht."
"I understand your frustration and this was not my intention."

"Leider kann ich Ihre Vorschläge nicht so einfach umsetzen."
"Unfortunately, I cannot implement your proposals so easily."

"Können wir vielleicht einen Kompromiss finden?"
"Can we maybe find a compromise?"

If the other person agrees, be sure to let them know your appreciation:

"Danke, dass du mit mir darüber reden willst. Hier ist mein Vorschlag:"
"Thank you for talking to me about this. Here is my proposal:"

Maybe the problem can't be resolved right away and a solution needs to be postponed:

"Leider werden wir uns hier im Moment nicht einig. Aber lass uns später noch einmal darüber reden."
"Unfortunately, we will not come to an agreement right now. But let us talk about this again later."

Then you can use some of the "meeting new people" phrases from last subchapter to get their phone number or arrange another conversation in the future!

Exercises

When trying to defuse a conflict in German, it is important to …

1. Excuse yourself for your behavior even if it isn't immediately clear to you what went wrong.
    a) true   b) false

2. Quickly offer a solution of your own before listening to the other party's proposal.
    a) true   b) false

3. Always try and fix the situation right away, don't postpone.
    a) true   b) false

Which of those phrases are formed correctly?

4. a) Entschuldige mir bitte   b) Entschuldigen Sie bitte
    c) Entschuldige bitte   d) Entschuldigen Sie bitte mich

5. a) Ich verstehe Ihren Ärger.
    b) Ich verstehe deinen Ärger.
    c) Ich verstehe Ärger.
    d) Ärger verstehe ich.

Chapter 6.5
Haggling and negotiating

Buying and trading are a big part of the social experience in any society and while prices are not up for negotiation in German supermarkets, there are many flea markets, garage sales and online auction platforms where you could negotiate a better price for something you would like to have. Some of the phrases you will learn in this subchapter could help you with that.

First of all, you want to know what stuff costs:

"Wie viel kostet das?"
"How much does that cost?"

"Können Sie mir den Preis hierfür nennen?"
"Can you tell me the price for this here?"

At this point you might be interested, but not yet satisfied with the price:

"Ich hätte Interesse, aber können wir nicht noch etwas am Preis machen?"
"I'd be interested, but can't we do something about the price still?"

"Was ist Ihr letzter Preis?"
"What's your best offer?"

Then you might get an offer that you would like to counter:

"Wie wäre es stattdessen mit 100 Euro?"
"How about 100 Euros instead?"

"Wie wäre es mit einem Rabatt, wenn ich mehrere Dinge kaufe?"
"How about a rebate if I buy several things?"

Eventually your wiggling room for price negotiations might be exhausted; at this point you could still try and score some other benefit:

"Würden Sie mir das für diesen Preis gratis liefern?"
"Would you consider free shipping at this price?"

After you have agreed on a price, you can ask for a receipt if it's something you bought in a physical store rather than online:

"Können Sie mir dafür eine Quittung geben?"
"Can you give me a receipt for that?"

Always keep in mind the rules for respectful and polite conversations you have learned in previous subchapters, too. A few more "Bitte" and "Danke" might be worth a few euros at the end of your negotiation!

Exercises

Identify the accurately constructed haggling phrases:

1. a) Wie viel kostet das?
    b) Wie viel kosten das?
    c) Was sind Kosten davon?
    d) Wie viele Kosten das?

2. a) Was ist letzte Preis?
    b) Was ist Ihr letzter Preis?
    c) Letzte Preis ist?
    d) Was ist Preis letzter?

3. a) Stattdessen wie wäre 100 Euro?
    b) Wie wäre es stattdessen mit 100 Euro?
    c) Wie stattdessen 100 Euro?
    d) Wie wären Sie stattdessen mit 100 Euro?

Which of the following statements is true?

4. There aren't many opportunities for haggling in Germany anyway.
    a) true   b) false

5. German rules for polite conversation also apply when haggling.
    a) true   b) false

Chapter 6.6
Business meetings

To conclude the chapter, we will delve into the business world and explore some sayings and phrases that will help you win hearts and minds during a meeting or conference.

We shall assume that you are not the moderator or leader of the meeting or conference, but a mere participant. In this case, how do you make yourself known if you actually do want to contribute something?

"Darf ich kurz unterbrechen?"
"May I briefly interrupt?"

"Ich habe etwas zum Thema beizutragen."
"I have something to contribute to the topic."

"Ich würde gern eine Idee mit Ihnen teilen."
"I would like to share an idea with you."

Maybe instead of contributing yourself, you would like to ask for clarification on some other person's input:

"Entschuldigung, ich habe eine Frage."
"Excuse me, I have a question."

"Könnten Sie das bitte genauer erläutern?"
"Could you explain this in more detail?"

"Könnten Sie das bitte noch einmal wiederholen?"
"Could you repeat this once again please?"

At some point, you might find yourself disagreeing with another participant's ideas and want to respectfully challenge him or propose a different point of view:

"Ihre Perspektive ist sehr interessant, aber ich habe einen Gegenvorschlag."
"Your perspective is very interesting, but I have a counter proposal."

"Ich kann Ihnen leider nicht zustimmen und erkläre gern, warum."
"I unfortunately cannot agree with and would like to explain why."

Over the course of the conversation, you may feel that people are wandering off topic or the point of the meeting is otherwise being missed. In this case, you may try and bring people back to the original purpose of the meeting:

"Wir sollten vielleicht zum ursprünglichen Thema zurückkehren."
"We should maybe return to the original topic."

"Wir sollten uns, glaube ich, auf andere Schwerpunkte konzentrieren."
"We should, I believe, focus on other themes."

Remember to be polite and respectful in your official business dealings, too.

Exercises

Which of the following business meeting phrases are accurately constructed?

1. a) Muss ich kurz unterbrechen?
    b) Soll ich kurz unterbrechen?
    c) Kann ich kurz unterbrechen?
    d) Darf ich kurz unterbrechen?

2. a) Bitte Sie erklären genauer.
    b) Erklären Sie bitte genauer.
    c) Genauer erklären Sie bitte.
    d) Sie erklären bitte genauer.

3. a) Können Sie das bitte wiederholen?
    b) Können Sie das wiederholen, bitte?
    c) Sie das wiederholen können, bitte?
    d) Bitte Sie das wiederholen können?

Which of the following statements are true?

4. German business culture is very direct and you should not waste time on pleasantries.
    a) true   b) false

5. You should address mostly ideas and not people directly in a German business meeting.
    a) true   b) false

Chapter 7.1
Separable verbs

These will be your last grammar lessons before we release you to venture out into the world of German and build up your vocabulary. In this subchapter, we will deal with separable verbs: verbs that take on a new meaning by adding a prefix.

The English language knows separable verbs as a linguistic import: there are many compound verbs that probably started out this way; for instance "start out" or "lift up" or "give in". But German has a whole system of adding certain prefixes to give words a new meaning. The list of these prefixes is long and generally the meaning is clear immediately (for instance, "holen" (fetch) can be combined with "zurück" (back) to produce "zurückholen" (retrieve)). You will now learn about three very common separable verb prefixes with some examples.

ab-

Attaching the prefix ab- to a verb gives it the additional connotation of something being removed or taken away. For example:

schneiden (cut) -> abschneiden (cut off)
wählen (vote) -> abwählen (vote out)
sagen (say) -> absagen (cancel, renege, decline)

auf-

This prefix adds the meaning of adding, opening or undoing something.

bauen (build) -> aufbauen (build up)
schließen (lock) -> aufschließen (unlock)
geben (give) -> aufgeben (give up)

ein-

Verbs combined with ein- gain the connotation that something is put in or into something else.

atmen (breathe) -> einatmen (breathe in)
steigen (climb) -> einsteigen (climb in)
zahlen (pay) -> einzahlen (pay in)

The reason these verbs are called separable is that they get separated from their prefix in their finite forms:

Er **baut** sein Unternehmen **auf**.
He is building up his company.

Sie **steigt** in ein Auto **ein**.
She climbs into a car.

If they stand with a modal verb, they do not get separated:

Er will sein Unternehmen **aufbauen**.
He wants to build up his company.

There are also some verbs that are compounded like separable ones, but do not experience the same separation in the sentence structure. For instance, verbs with the prefix miss- (fail to, do wrong) stick together:

Ich **missverstehe** vielleicht deine Frage.
Perhaps I understand your question poorly.

And then there is a third category of compounded verbs that are sometimes separable and sometimes not; to make matters worse, the separated and non-separated versions of the verb tend to have different meanings, too. This tends to be true for verbs compounded with um- (around, to the ground):

Ich **umfahre** den Baum.
I drive around the tree.

Ich **fuhr** den Baum **um**.
I knocked down the tree while driving.

Very different meanings there! This is another case where you will have to memorize the distinctions and exceptions as you build up your vocabulary.

Exercises

Which of the following statements are true?

1. All compound verbs in German are separable.
    a) true   b) false

2. All compound verbs in German fall into either the separable or non-separable category.
    a) true   b) false

3. Compound verbs in German can sometimes take on different meanings depending on whether they are separated or not.
    a) true   b) false

Identify the correctly constructed phrases:

4. a) Wir abwählen den Präsident.
    b) Wir wählen den Präsident ab.
    c) Wir den Präsident abwählen.
    d) Wir wählen ab den Präsident.

5. a) Ich aufpasse auf mich.
    b) Ich mich aufpasse.
    c) Ich passe auf mich auf.
    d) Ich auf mich aufpassen.

Chapter 7.2
When to use genitive or dative

This distinction tends to be tricky in some cases even for native German speakers. Let's briefly remember the purpose of the dative and genitive cases: the dative case marks the indirect object in a sentence, someone or something that is being acted upon or that is receiving something, whereas the genitive case indicates ownership.

Paul's car looks great.
Pauls Auto sieht toll aus. (genitive)

The car was given to Paul.
Das Auto wurde **Paul** gegeben. (dative)

This would be quite straightforward, except for the problem that you can transform all genitive cases into dative cases in German when adding the preposition "von":

Paul's car looks great.
Das Auto **von Paul** sieht toll aus.

While this tends to work decent enough with names that don't carry articles, it ends up sounding unsophisticated with article-carrying nouns or names that do use articles; for instance, the country of Turkey is known in German as "die Türkei" and the following sentence would be considered not very good German, although grammatically correct:

Turkey's economy is doing good.
Die Wirtschaft **von der Türkei** läuft gut.

So, to avoid looking boorish, stick to these two rules when constructing your genitives:

1. If it's a name without an article, feel free to either use the "s" ending and construct a proper genitive or the "von" construction with dative:
   Deutschland**s** Wirtschaft läuft gut.
   Die Wirtschaft **von** Deutschland läuft gut.

2. If it's a noun or a name that carries an article, use the proper genitive article "des" or "der":
   Die Wirtschaft **der** Türkei läuft gut.
   Das Geschäft **des** Manns läuft gut.

Exercises

Identify the properly formed **genitives**:

1. a) das Haus von dem Paul   b) Pauls Haus
   c) das Haus von Paul   d) Haus des Pauls

2. a) das Manns Auto   b) das Auto von Mann
    c) das Auto des Manns   d) Auto von Manns

3. a) Türkeis Autos   a) Autos von die Türkei
    c) Autos Türkeis   d) Autos der Türkei

Which of the following statements is true?

4. You can technically turn all genitives into datives in German.
    a) true   b) false

5. It is considered more sophisticated to use datives.
    a) true   b) false

Chapter 7.3
Difference between new and old spelling rules

In this last subchapter and in fact final lesson of the book, we will look into how some spelling regulations in German were changed in the recent past and what the old spelling looked like, and we will do this because many people even in formal settings still cling to the old rules, sometimes as a fashion statement. So lest you get confused by old-timey rules, let's familiarize ourselves with them.

The most important and wide-ranging changes of this spelling reform from 1996 concerns the sharp S, the letter ß that you learned in the very beginning of the book. In the old spelling, the letter ß was generally used as a stand-in in all words with a drawn-out S even if they were short-spoken and not "sharp", for instance:

Schloss (castle) -> Schloß
Genuss (enjoyment) -> Genuß
muss (must) -> muß

In the new spelling regime, ß only appears anymore in words with a really long-spoken ß, for instance "Spaß" (fun) or Gruß (greeting).

A number of people still stick to the old usage of ß, however, and you will encounter a lot of "daß", "muß" or "Kuß" (kiss) variations especially in informal writing. Don't be alarmed: these words have the exact same meaning as their cousins with a double S; they are just old-fashioned.

Another change that came with this reform concerned the topic of **compound words**, which you learned about in a previous chapter. Previously, when these compound words would end up connecting three identical consonants, one was removed for the sake of readability, but now this is not true anymore:

Schritt (step) + Tempo (speed) = Schritttempo (walking pace, walking speed)
Nuss (nut) + Schokolade (chocolate) = Nussschokolade (nutty chocolate)

Lastly, and this is somewhat annoying for new learners of the language, certain spellings from Greek and Latin loan words that were spelled almost identically in English were "Germanised". This particularly concerns the "ph" in words like "geography":

Geographie (old spelling) -> Geografie (new spelling)

On the other hand, the "ph" was maintained in certain other words like "Philosophie", so this reform partially introduced more irregularity into the language. Many people still stick to the "ph" spelling in all Latin and Greek loan words and it is rare to see someone actually use a spelling variant like "Saxofon" in written language even though it's technically correct now.

Exercises

Which of these words are constructed according to the new spelling rules?

1. a) dass   b) Genuss
    c) Spaß   d) muß

2. a) Fluss   b) Gruß
    c) Haß   d) daß

Which of the following statements are true?

3. Everyone is required to follow the new spelling rules and everyone does.
    a) true   b) false

4. If you build a compound word, it can now contain a sequence of three or more of the same consonants.
    a) true   b) false

5. All the "ph"s in loan words were replaced by "f"s under the new spelling rules.
    a) true   b) false

Answer key

Chapter 1.1

1: a), b)
2: b), d)
3: c), d)
4: b), d)
5: a), d)

Chapter 1.2

1: b), c)
2: c), d)
3: d)
4: d)
5: a), c)

Chapter 1.3

1: a)
2: a)
3: c), d)
4: c), d)
5: a), b), c), d)

Chapter 1.4

1: b)
2: c)
3: b)
4: c)
5: b)

Chapter 1.5

1: d)
2: b), d)
3: a)
4: b)
5: b)

Chapter 1.6

1: a), b), d)

2: b), c), d)
3: a), d)
4: d)
5: c)

Chapter 2.1

1: a), d)
2: b), c), d)
3: a), c), d)
4: a), c)
5: c), d)

Chapter 2.2

1: c)
2: a)
3: a)
4: c)
5: a), c), d)

Chapter 2.3

1: b)
2: a)
3: b)
4: a), b), d)
5: a), b), c), d)

Chapter 2.4

1: b), d)
2: a), b), d)
3: b), c), d)
4: a), b)
5: a), b), c)

Chapter 3.1

1: a), d)
2: a), d)
3: c), d)

4: a), b)
5: a)

Chapter 3.2

1: c)
2: a), c)
3: a), b), c)
4: b), d)
5: b)

Chapter 3.3

1: a), c)
2: a), d)
3: a), c), d)
4: a)
5: b)

Chapter 3.4

1: a), c)
2: b)
3: b), d)
4: b)
5: b); it should be „40 Prozent VON Amerika lebt rural"

Chapter 4.1

1: a), d)
2: a), c)
3: a), c)
4: a)
5: b); it would have to be „führe" and „würde ausmachen"

Chapter 4.2

1: b)
2: c), d)
3: b), c), d)
4: a), d)
5: b), c)

Chapter 4.3

1: c), d)
2: c), d)
3: sometimes d)
4: b)
5: a)

Chapter 4.4

1: b)
2: b), d)
3: a), d)
4: a)
5: b)

Chapter 4.5

1: b), c)
2: a), d)
3: c)
4: a), d)
5: b), c), d)

Chapter 4.6

1: c), d)
2: b), c)
3: b)
4: b)
5: a), c), d)

Chapter 4.7

1: c), d)
2: a)
3: a), c)
4: b)
5) a)

Chapter 5.1

1: b)

2: c)
3: a)
4: a), c)
5: d)

Chapter 5.2

1: a), c)
2: b)
3: b, d)
4: a), c), d)
5: c), d)

Chapter 5.3

1: b), c)
2: a), c)
3: c), d)
4: b), d)
5: b)

Chapter 5.4

1: c)
2: c)
3: b), d)
4: a)
5: b)

Chapter 5.5

1: b)
2: a)
3) b)
4: b), d)
5: c), d)

Chapter 6.1

1: b)
2: a)
3: b)

4: a)
5: a)

Chapter 6.2

1: c)
2: b)
3: b)
4: b)
5: a)

Chapter 6.3

1: a), d)
2: c), d)
3: a), b), d)
4: c)
5: d)

Chapter 6.4

1: a)
2: b)
3: b)
4: b), c)
5: a), b)

Chapter 6.5

1: a)
2: b)
3: b)
4: b)
5: a)

Chapter 6.6

1: c), d)
2: b)
3: a), b)
4: b)
5: b)

Chapter 7.1

1: b)
2: b)
3: a)
4: b)
5: c)

Chapter 7.2

1: b)
2: c)
3: d)
4: a)
5: b)

Chapter 7.3

1: a), b), c)
2: a), b)
3: b)
4: a)
5: b)

German Phrasebook For Beginners

Beginners

Learn Common Phrases In Context With Explanations For Everyday Use and Travel

Worldwide Nomad

Introduction

In the intricate tapestry of languages spoken globally, few are as captivating, enigmatic, and, above all, practical as the German language. With its melodic rhythm, refined structure, and diverse cultural heritage, German stands not merely as a mode of communication but as a portal to comprehend a nation deeply rooted in tradition and innovation.

Willkommen to Learn Conversational German, a journey through the heart and soul of this extraordinary language. Whether you're a prospective traveler, a business professional eager to broaden your horizons, or simply someone enchanted by the beauty of German culture, this book is your key to unlocking the door to speaking and understanding conversational German.

This book is meticulously crafted with the aim of empowering you with essential skills and knowledge to engage in meaningful conversations in German. It caters to learners of all levels, from absolute beginners to those seeking to enhance their existing German language skills. By the end of this book, you will not only have a solid grasp of conversational German but also a deeper appreciation for German culture and customs.

Have you ever envisioned strolling through the charming streets of Berlin, Vienna, Zurich, Munich, Hamburg, or Frankfurt? Have you ever dreamed of immersing yourself in the rich cultural history of the German-speaking world? Conversational German is your passport to such experiences. This book is purposefully designed.

First and foremost, it seeks to equip you with practical communication skills. Whether you find yourself ordering your favorite German dish at a local restaurant, seeking directions, or engaging in casual banter with locals, this book provides you with the ability to communicate effectively in everyday situations.

Secondly, this book offers cultural insights. It delves into the intricacies of German culture, values, and customs, enriching your interactions and fostering meaningful connections with native speakers. Understanding the cultural context of the language will not only enhance your proficiency but also deepen your appreciation of German culture.

This book is also tailored to boost your confidence in speaking German. It achieves this by gradually introducing you to the language's fundamentals and guiding you through practical exercises and real-life dialogues. As you progress through the chapters, you will find yourself becoming more comfortable and proficient in expressing yourself in German.

When it comes to German, a language renowned for its beauty and global influence, the initial intimidation can be overwhelming. However, fear not—this book is meticulously written to transform your language-learning journey into an enjoyable and highly effective experience.

In addition to linguistic proficiency, we will offer invaluable cultural insights. By exploring the customs, traditions, and etiquette that shape both the language and its native speakers, you will gain a deeper appreciation of German culture. This cultural understanding will not only enrich your interactions but also foster a sense of respect and connection with the people you communicate with.

The ability to navigate real-life scenarios is an essential component of language learning. This book equips you with the necessary tools to excel in practical situations by providing dialogues and vocabulary tailored to everyday conversations. Whether you're ordering your favorite German dish at a restaurant or seeking directions on the bustling streets of Germany, you'll be well-prepared for your interactions, ensuring that your experiences in Germany are both enjoyable and enriching.

Now that you possess the essential linguistic tools from the German Grammar book, it's time to apply them to real-world situations. From ordering delectable dishes at a local restaurant to seeking directions through unfamiliar streets and engaging in casual chit-chat, we will prepare you for the myriad of everyday scenarios you may encounter while exploring Germany.

Language and culture are inextricably intertwined, forming the essence of a nation's identity. You'll gain profound insights into German customs, traditions, and social etiquette. This cultural understanding ensures that your conversations not only maintain linguistic accuracy but also reflect a deep respect for the rich tapestry of German culture.

Building upon the sturdy foundation established earlier, you'll be introduced to an expansive array of vocabulary. You'll acquire words and phrases spanning various topics, empowering you to engage in diverse conversations and express your thoughts and emotions with precision.

Throughout this book, you'll find that the German language is not just a means of communication; it's a key that opens doors to a rich and vibrant culture. So, let's embark on this adventure together. Ready your German alphabet characters, sharpen your curiosity, and let's set sail into the world of Conversational German!

Chapter 1
Greeting in German

The Basics

Introducing yourself in a German-speaking country involves expressing courtesy, directness, and a sincere interest in building connections. Unlike some other European countries, especially in the north of Germany, people may initially come across as more reserved and direct. While excessive displays of warmth may not be as common, Germans appreciate straightforwardness and honesty in communication.

Here's a brief guide to help you navigate introductions in a German setting, along with a useful phrase to initiate a positive first conversation:

Start with a Greeting

Initiate the interaction with a courteous greeting. Whether you're addressing a friend or meeting someone for the first time, the initial greeting should be polite and direct. The straightforwardness you convey during the greeting sets the tone for the rest of the conversation.

The energy you convey during the greeting sets the tone for the rest of the conversation. If you want to make friends in Germany, don't be afraid to be sociable. In many German-speaking regions, people commonly use handshakes as a form of greeting, particularly in formal settings. However, among friends and acquaintances, hugs or cheek kisses might be more prevalent. It's important to note that the level of physical contact can vary by region and individual preferences, and it may initially feel unfamiliar or uncomfortable.

Embracing these cultural nuances in greetings is a valuable part of integrating into German social interactions.

Use Formal Titles

If you're in a formal setting, it is polite to address people using their titles and last names until given permission to use first names. "Herr" (Mr.) and "Frau" (Mrs.) are commonly used titles before the person's last name.

Some formal greetings are:

Guten Morgen Herr Müller

Good morning, Mr. Müller

Guten Tag Frau Meier

Good afternoon, Mrs. Meier

Es freut mich sehr, Sie kennenzulernen, Herr und Frau Schneider.

Very pleased to meet you, Mr. and Mrs. Schneider.

Express Politeness

Manners and politeness are highly valued in German culture. Germans generally appreciate directness, punctuality, and a certain level of formality in social interactions. Here are some key aspects of manners and politeness in Germany:

Greetings: Greetings are an important aspect of German etiquette. A firm handshake and maintaining eye contact are common in both professional and social settings. When entering a room or a small group, it's customary to greet each person individually. Titles such as "Herr" (Mr.) or "Frau" (Mrs.) are often used, especially in formal situations.

Table Manners: Table manners are significant in German culture. When dining, it's polite to keep your hands on the table (but not your elbows) and wait until everyone is served before starting to eat. Saying "Guten Appetit" (enjoy your meal) before eating is a common practice.

Addressing Others: Using formal titles and last names is customary when addressing people you are not well-acquainted with or in professional settings. As relationships become more familiar, individuals might switch to using first names.

Apologies and Thank You: Apologizing and expressing gratitude are essential aspects of politeness. If you accidentally bump into someone or make a mistake, a sincere apology is expected. Similarly, saying "Danke" (thank you) for favors or assistance is common.

Privacy: Germans value their privacy, and it's considered polite to respect personal space. People may be more reserved in sharing personal information, especially in initial interactions.

Formality in Language: The German language reflects a certain level of formality through the use of formal and informal pronouns ("du" and "Sie"). In professional settings or when addressing someone of higher rank or authority, using the formal "Sie" is often preferred.

Gift-Giving: When presenting gifts, it's customary to open them in the presence of the giver. Additionally, expressing appreciation for the gift is important.

Remember that while these general guidelines provide insight into German manners and politeness, individual preferences may vary. It's always beneficial to observe and adapt to the specific social norms of the situation and the people involved.If you are eating at a table, always ask for permission to.

Be Mindful of Time

Punctuality is a strongly emphasized aspect of German culture, and being on time is considered a sign of respect and professionalism. Even though the trains are very rarely on time, it is expected of you to be not only on time for an appointment, but better yet, be early. Here are some key points to understand about punctuality in Germany:

Meeting Deadlines: Germans are known for their strong work ethic, and meeting deadlines is a crucial aspect of professional life. Whether it's a work project, a business meeting, or a social gathering, being punctual is seen as a demonstration of reliability and commitment.

Social Punctuality: Punctuality extends beyond the workplace into social and casual settings. If you are invited to someone's home for a meal or a gathering, arriving on time is expected. Germans place a high value on planning and organization, and tardiness can be perceived as a lack of consideration for others' time.

Public Transportation: Germans also expect punctuality when it comes to public transportation. Trains and buses run on tight schedules, and it's common for people to plan their journeys with precision. Being late for public transport is not only inconvenient for oneself but can also disrupt the schedules of others. However, trains are rarely on time, but the bus or Straßenbahn (tram) is most of the times very punctual.

Consequences of Tardiness: In professional settings, being consistently late or missing deadlines can have negative consequences. It may affect your professional reputation and relationships with colleagues. In social situations, arriving significantly late without a valid reason may be seen as disrespectful.

Communication about Delays: If, for any reason, you anticipate being late, it is considered courteous to inform the relevant parties as soon as possible. This applies to both professional and social commitments. Germans appreciate open communication and understanding of unforeseen circumstances.

Cultural Norms: Punctuality is deeply ingrained in German culture, and there is a general expectation that others will be punctual as well. This cultural norm helps maintain efficiency in various aspects of life, from business transactions to social events.

It's important to note that while punctuality is a cultural norm in Germany, flexibility is sometimes permitted for casual or informal gatherings among close friends. However, in professional and formal settings, being on time is a clear expectation. Adjusting to this cultural practice can contribute positively to your interactions and relationships in Germany.

Engage in Small Talk

Small talk in Germany is generally purposeful and seen as a way to establish connections before diving into more substantive conversations. It is valued for its efficiency, often focusing on relevant topics like the weather. Germans appreciate concise and direct communication, avoiding superficial or insincere conversations. In professional settings, small talk tends to be more formal, while in casual settings small talk may adopt a more relaxed demeanor. Germans value personal space, so it's advisable to gauge familiarity before discussing personal matters. Good listening skills are appreciated, and authenticity is key in small talk interactions. Overall, understanding the cultural context and adapting to the direct communication style contributes to successful small talk in Germany.

Some useful phrases are:

Wie geht's? (formal)

Wie geht es Ihnen? (informal)

How are you?

Wie war dein Wochenende? (formal)

Wie war Ihr Wochenende? (informal)

How was your weekend?

Wie geht es deiner Familie? (formal)

Wie geht es Ihrer Familie? (informal)

How is your family doing?

Was machst du gerne in deiner Freizeit? (formal)

Was machen Sie gerne in Ihrer Freizeit? (informal)

What do you like doing in your free time?

Use Formal Language

As we saw in the previous questions, there is a formal and an informal way to treat others. The formal way is using the pronoun Sie. The informal way uses the pronouns du.

Du bist mein bester Freund.

You are my best friend.

Du bist hier.

You are here.

Du arbeitest in der Schule.

You work in the school.

Until you are familiar with the level of formality in a particular setting, it's advisable to use formal language, that is, using Sie to address others. This is especially true when addressing older individuals or those in positions of authority.

Once you have established a rapport with others, they may start using the pronoun *du*, and they will also ask you to do the same.

Learn Basic Phrases in German

While many Germans speak English, making an effort to communicate in German will be always be appreciated. If people notice you are trying to use German, they will help you, correct you and teach you. It is like having free German lessons every time you speak.

Show Genuine Interest

In German culture, people appreciate genuine interest, but value efficiency and directness in conversation. While they may engage in small talk, it tends to be more purposeful and concise. Germans may prefer to keep conversations concise and focused after a simple greeting, and they often appreciate getting to the point in discussions.

Participate in Cultural Customs

If there are specific cultural customs or traditions in Germany, make an effort to participate. In fact, locals may expect and appreciate your participation, even participating in local activities. Whether it's joining in for a traditional meal, attending local events, or partaking in a dance, active involvement builds rapport and strengthens relationships. While Germans won't be offended if you decline, seizing these opportunities to engage demonstrates your enthusiasm to enjoy, learn, and have a fantastic time!

Keep in mind that every country and region in Germany has its own unique customs and nuances, so it's crucial to be adaptable and observant. The key is to approach introductions with respect, an open mind, and a willingness to embrace the local culture.

Chapter 2
Transportation

Now, let's delve into essential vocabulary and phrases every traveler needs on their journey through Germany. Join us as we explore the vibrant world of transportation in this chapter, uncovering the everyday expressions woven into the German language.

These phrases will empower you to effortlessly navigate every corner of Germany, from bustling city streets to tranquil rural roads. Mastering them opens the door to communication with locals, seeking assistance, and inquiring about bus, train, or metro fares, enriching your overall travel experience.

Keep in mind that transportation in German-speaking countries serves as a bridge between movement and cultural identity shaping sociological and economic perspectives.

As we navigate the linguistic landscape, we'll encounter phrases that encapsulate the essence of travel, offering insights into customs, habits, and attitudes surrounding transportation in German-speaking regions. Whether you're a language enthusiast, a traveler eager to connect with locals, or simply curious about the idiomatic expressions coloring everyday conversations, this chapter invites you to explore the linguistic crossroads where language and transportation intersect.

Are you ready for this linguistic journey? Join us as we unveil the meanings behind phrases that go beyond words, painting vivid pictures of the diverse modes of transportation and how they're uniquely embedded in the German-speaking world. From the rhythmic cadence of urban commutes to the unhurried pace of rural travels, each phrase is a snapshot of the cultural landscapes shaping the German language.

So, buckle up, hop on board, and let us be your passport to the captivating world of transportation idioms in German. Through the lens of language, we embark on a fascinating exploration of the expressions bridging the gap between where we are and where we want to go. Before we dive into the phrases and vocabulary, here's some information that will prove valuable.

Trains

Welcome to the heart of Europe, where an efficient and extensive railway network awaits to guide you through the breathtaking scenery and dynamic urban centers of Germany. In this chapter, we'll unravel the secrets of traveling by train in Germany, offering you essential insights for an enriching experience.

Trains hold a special place in the German transportation system, forming the backbone that seamlessly connects cities, towns, and regions. Unlike some countries where train travel might be limited, Germany's extensive and well-connected railway system allows you to explore the country comfortably and efficiently.

Germany boasts a variety of trains catering to diverse travel preferences. From high-speed ICE trains connecting major cities to regional trains connecting smaller communities, you have a range of options. Local trains, or S-Bahn, operate within urban areas, providing easy access to different districts.

The regional and intercity trains seamlessly connect diverse regions, allowing you to experience the country's beauty. Whether you're captivated by the medieval allure of Bavaria or the cosmopolitan flair of Berlin, the train system ensures seamless travel.

Ticketing is simple and convenient, with options to purchase tickets at stations, online, or through the Deutsche Bahn website. If you're planning on traveling frequently, consider purchasing a rail pass.

The trains in Germany are designed for passenger comfort. Expect clean and well-maintained carriages with comfortable seating and free Wi-Fi to stay connected while you travel.

While Germans, especially in public spaces like trains, generally prefer personal space and quietness, it doesn't mean you can't strike up a friendly conversation. Be mindful of your surroundings and the preferences of fellow travelers, and you'll find that many Germans are open to brief interactions.

Germany is renowned for its picturesque landscapes, and the train routes showcase the country's beauty. Consider taking scenic routes like the Rhine Valley Railway or the Black Forest Railway for an immersive experience.

Most train personnel speak English, but learning a few German phrases can enhance your experience. "Fahrkarte" means ticket, and "Bahnhof" is the train station. Simple expressions like "Bitte" (please) and "Danke" (thank you) go a long way.

Metros and Subways

Metro systems are a prevalent feature in several major German cities, contributing to efficient and reliable public transportation. Cities like Berlin, Munich, Hamburg, Cologne, and Frankfurt have well-established U-Bahn (underground railway) networks, providing comprehensive coverage within the urban centers and extending to suburban areas.

Additionally, cities such as Nuremberg, Dortmund, Essen, and Stuttgart also feature metro or subway systems, further enhancing the overall efficiency of public transportation in Germany.

It's worth noting that almost every larger city boasts a well-developed network of trams and buses, complementing the metro systems. These tram and bus networks offer additional flexibility for getting around, providing convenient options for both residents and visitors. Whether you're navigating through bustling city streets or exploring suburban areas, Germany's public transportation infrastructure is designed to meet diverse travel needs.

Taxis and Ride-Sharing Services

Taxis are a common and regulated mode of transportation in Germany, readily identifiable by their distinctive colors and rooftop signs displaying the company's name. While taxis can be hailed on the street, designated taxi stands are ubiquitous throughout cities. These stands serve as convenient points for finding a taxi or you can opt to pre-book through taxi companies or apps.

Taxis operate on a metered fare system, including a base charge, distance traveled, and waiting time. The rates are regulated, and it is customary for the meter to be used during the journey. Payment for taxi services can be made in cash or major credit cards, and it's advisable to confirm payment options with the driver beforehand.

In urban areas, taxis are readily available, offering a reliable means of transportation. The convenience of taxis lies in their visibility and accessibility, making them a popular choice for both locals and visitors navigating city streets.

Ride-sharing services like Uber are mostly only available in larger cities like Berlin, Hamburg, or Munich. In addition to Uber, other ride-sharing services complying with German regulations may be available. Users can easily request rides, track drivers, and make cashless payments through mobile apps.

Common Phrases and Vocabulary

Common Phrases	Translation
What bus route takes me to …?	Welche Buslinie bringt mich nach …?
What metro line takes me to …?	Welche U-Bahn-Linie bringt mich nach…?
How frequent is the bus?	Wie häufig fährt der Bus?
How frequent is the train/metro?	Wie häufig fährt der Zug/die U-Bahn?
How much is the bus fare?	Wie viel kostet der Bus?
How much is the taxi fare?	Wie hoch ist der Taxipreis?
How much is the metro fare?	Wie viel kostet die U-Bahn?
How much is the train fare?	Wie viel kostet der Zug?
I need help.	Ich brauche Hilfe.
Where can I take the bus/metro/train/taxi?	Wo kann ich den Bus/die U-Bahn/den Zug/das Taxi nehmen?
Where can I buy a card for the bus/metro/train?	Wo kann ich eine Karte für Bus/U-Bahn/Bahn kaufen?
I want to add credit to my card.	Ich möchte meiner Karte Guthaben hinzufügen.
Where do I have to get off if I need to go to …?	Wo muss ich aussteigen, wenn ich nach … muss?

What is the closest station?	Welcher Bahnhof ist am nächsten?
Where do I need to transfer?	Wohin muss ich umsteigen?
Where can I transfer?	Wohin kann ich umsteigen?
What time does the bus service begin?	Wann beginnt der Busverkehr?
What time does the bus service finish?	Um wie viel Uhr endet der Busverkehr?
Could you tell me how to get to …?	Könnten Sie mir sagen, wie ich dorthin komme?
Am I close to …?	Bin ich in der Nähe von…?
Can I sit here?	Kann ich hier sitzen?
Yes, of course!	Ja natürlich!
No, it is taken.	Nein, es ist vergeben.
Where is the hospital?	Wo ist das Krankenhaus?
I need to go to a hospital.	Ich muss in ein Krankenhaus.
Where is the police station?	Wo ist die Polizei Station?
Where do I exit the station?	Wo verlasse ich den Bahnhof?
What platform do I need if I am going to …?	Welche Plattform benötige ich, wenn ich nach … möchte?
Where can I get a map of the metro lines?	Wo bekomme ich eine Karte für die U-Bahn?
Where can I get a map of the bus lines?	Wo bekomme ich eine Karte für den Bus?
Where is the restroom?	Wo ist die Toilette?
How long does the bus take to get to …?	Wie lange dauert die Fahrt mit dem Bus nach …?
How long does the train take to get to …?	Wie lange dauert die Fahrt mit dem Zug nach …?
How long does the metro take to get to …?	Wie lange braucht die U-Bahn bis …?
Can I get there by walking?	Kann ich zu Fuß dorthin gelangen?
What route is this bus?	Welche Route fährt dieser Bus?
What line is this train?	Auf welcher Linie fährt dieser Zug?
What time is it?	Wie spät ist es?
What time will we arrive?	Wann werden wir ankommen?
Where can I buy one ticket?	Wo kann ich ein Ticket kaufen?
Can I pay with spare money or do I need to buy a card?	Kann ich mit Bargeld bezahlen oder muss ich eine Karte kaufen?
Can I buy a weekly/monthly/unlimited pass?	Kann ich eine Wochen-/Monats-/unbegrenzte Karte kaufen?
Is there a student discount?	Gibt es einen Studentenrabatt?
Where can I find an available taxi?	Wo finde ich ein verfügbares Taxi?
Where is the taxi terminal?	Wo ist der Taxistand?
Where are you going?	Wo gehst du hin?

What is your destination?	Was ist Ihr Ziel?
Please, take me to [location].	Bitte bringen Sie mich zu [Standort].
I need to go to [location].	Ich muss nach [Standort].
How long will it take to get to [location]?	Wie lange wird es dauern, bis ich [Standort] erreiche?
What is the fare for a trip to [location]?	Wie hoch ist der Fahrpreis für eine Fahrt nach [Ort]?
Can you drive faster?	Könnten Sie schneller fahren?
Can you drive slower?	Könnten Sie langsamer fahren?
Can you turn up volume?	Können Sie die Lautstärke erhöhen?
Can you turn down volume?	Können Sie die Lautstärke verringern?
Can you change the radio station?	Können Sie den Radiosender wechseln?
Can you turn on the radio?	Können Sie das Radio einschalten?
Can you turn off the radio?	Können Sie das Radio ausschalten?
Is it difficult to catch a taxi in this part of the city?	Ist es schwierig, in diesem Teil der Stadt ein Taxi zu bekommen?
There is a lot of traffic.	Dort ist viel Verkehr.
Can I pay with a card or cash?	Kann ich mit Karte oder Bargeld bezahlen?
Please, take this route.	Bitte nehmen Sie diesen Weg.
Please, use the GPS.	Bitte nutzen Sie das GPS.
Please, open the window.	Bitte öffne das Fenster.
Please, close the window.	Bitte schließe das Fenster.
Can you help me with my luggage?	Können Sie mir mit meinem Gepäck helfen?
Can you turn on the AC?	Können Sie die Klimaanlage einschalten?
Can you turn off the AC?	Können Sie die Klimaanlage ausschalten?
Please, open the trunk.	Bitte öffnen Sie den Kofferraum.
I'll pay with a card.	Ich bezahle mit Karte.
I'll pay with cash.	Ich bezahle mit Bargeld.
You can drop me off here.	Sie können mich hier absetzen.
You can drop me off there.	Sie können mich dort absetzen.
You can drop me off in the corner.	Sie können mich in der Ecke absetzen.
I would like to go to the airport.	Ich würde gerne zum Flughafen fahren.
I would like to go to the museum.	Ich würde gerne ins Museum gehen.
I would like to go to downtown.	Ich würde gerne in die Innenstadt gehen.
I would like to go to the hotel …	Ich würde gerne ins Hotel gehen …
I'll get off here.	Ich werde hier aussteigen.
I'm sorry, can you wait for me a couple of minutes?	Es tut mir leid, können Sie ein paar Minuten auf mich warten?

How long will it take to get to my destination?	Wie lange wird es dauern, bis ich mein Ziel erreiche?
How can I get to [location] from here?	Wie komme ich von hier aus nach [Standort]?
What time is rush hour?	Wann ist Hauptverkehrszeit?
Can I have your card for future trips?	Kann ich Ihre Karte für zukünftige Reisen haben?
Can you stop by the supermarket on the way back?	Können Sie auf dem Rückweg noch beim Supermarkt anhalten?
How long have you been a driver and what places do you recommend in the city?	Seit wann sind Sie Taxifahrer und welche Orte in der Stadt empfehlen Sie?
Is this part of the city safe?	Ist dieser Teil der Stadt sicher?
Until what time do you drive?	Bis wann fahren Sie?
Let me know when I can get off.	Lassen Sie mich wissen, wann ich aussteigen kann.
Do you have a phone charger?	Haben Sie ein Telefonladegerät?
Please, take me to the downtown area.	Bitte bringen Sie mich in die Innenstadt.
Please, take me to the downtown bus terminal.	Bitte bringen Sie mich zum Busbahnhof in der Innenstadt.
Please, stop at the next gas station.	Bitte halten Sie an der nächsten Tankstelle an.
I can walk from here.	Ich kann von hier aus laufen.
Thank you for bringing me home.	Danke, dass du mich nach Hause gebracht hast.
Have a nice day/evening/night.	Hab einen schönen Tag/Abend/Nacht.

Vocabulary	Translation
Good morning!	Guten Morgen!
Good afternoon!	Guten Tag!
Good evening!	Guten Abend!
Good night!	Gute Nacht!
Metro/train station	U-Bahnhof/Bahnhof
Metro/train Terminal	U-Bahn-/Bahnterminal
Fare	Fahrpreis
Map	Karte
Transfers	Umsteigen
Departures	Abflüge
Arrivals	Ankünfte
Schedule	Zeitplan
Restroom	Toilette
Elevator	Aufzug

North	Norden
South	Süd
East	Ost
West	Westen
Avenue	Allee
Street	Straße
Boulevard	Boulevard
Cul de sac	Sackgasse
Cross the Street	Die Straße überqueren
Pedestrians' bridge	Fußgängerbrücke
Traffic light	Ampel
Far	Weit
Close, near	Nah
Distance	Distanz
Car	Auto
Bicycle	Fahrrad
Free Admission	Freier Eintritt
Discount	Rabatt
Children's Fare	Kindertarif

Chapter 3
Accommodation, Hotels and Airbnb in Germany

The hospitality industry in Germany is renowned for its warm and attentive service, ensuring that you are always treated like an esteemed guest in environments that promise a memorable and comfortable stay. Exploring accommodations in Germany invites you to immerse yourself in diverse cultures, where a nuanced understanding of cultural intricacies and etiquettes becomes indispensable for forging meaningful connections.

Beyond providing a mere place to rest and store your belongings, the German hospitality sector offers a supportive network committed to enhancing your overall experience during your stay. Those employed in this industry serve as your initial link to local culture and, importantly, stand ready to assist you in navigating any situation you might encounter. Whether you require additional amenities or seek recommendations for a hidden gem of a restaurant known only to locals, the individuals working in your hotel or your Airbnb host are the right people to approach for assistance.

What to expect and what to offer?

Expect genuine respect and courtesy during your stay in Germany, and reciprocate these values, as locals rightfully expect the same. Respect and courtesy are foundational in German cultures, and embracing these values is crucial when interacting with hotel staff, hosts, and fellow guests. Beyond mere transactions, these cultural pillars establish the groundwork for authentic connections and positive experiences throughout your stay.

Ensure you're not labeled as the person who disregards saying 'guten Morgen,' 'guten Tag,' 'guten Abend,' 'bitte,' or 'danke.' While omitting these expressions may not alter their attitude towards you, embodying kindness is a universally expected value in every interaction.

For a more profound immersion into these cultural values, consider seeking out family-owned hotels. Though smaller in scale than other accommodations, the opportunity to interact with owners and staff simultaneously offers a unique perspective on how, irrespective of position, power, or wealth, everyone treats others with respect and courtesy. This dynamic fosters connections with locals in ways that distinguish German cultures from other parts of the world.

Now, let's learn!

In this guide, we will delve into the intricacies of German hospitality, providing insights into the unique customs and expectations that shape the guest experience. By acquainting yourself with the language of hospitality, you will not only navigate the world of accommodations with confidence but also contribute to the rich tapestry of cultural exchange.

Let's explore phrases, questions, and vocabulary tailored to the world of hotels and Airbnb stays in Germany. By the end of this comprehensive exploration, you will possess the knowledge and language skills necessary to navigate the intricate and diverse landscape of accommodations with cultural sensitivity, ensuring that your journey is not just a physical one but also a cultural adventure that enriches your understanding of the places you visit.

Common Phrases	Translation
May I have the name for the reservation?	Darf ich den Namen für die Reservierung haben?
My reservation is for [Your Name].	Meine Reservierung gilt für [Ihren Namen].
I'm here to check in.	Ich bin hier, um einzuchecken.
I'm here to check out.	Ich bin hier, um auszuchecken.
What time is the check in?	Wann ist der Check-in?
What time is the check out?	Wann ist der Check-out?
Can I have an early check in?	Kann ich früher einchecken?
Can I check out early?	Kann ich früher auschecken?
Can I have a late check out?	Kann ich später auschecken?
Please, confirm my reservation.	Bitte bestätigen Sie meine Reservierung.
Can I pay with a debit card?	Kann ich mit einer Debitkarte bezahlen?
Can I pay with my credit card miles?	Kann ich mit meinen Kreditkartenmeilen bezahlen?
Can I pay with my credit card points?	Kann ich mit meinen Kreditkartenpunkten bezahlen?
What documents do you need?	Welche Unterlagen benötigen Sie?
Can I have my documents back?	Kann ich meine Unterlagen zurückbekommen?
Here you have my passport.	Hier haben Sie meinen Pass.
Do you have room service?	Haben Sie Zimmerservice?
Is there room service every day?	Gibt es jeden Tag Zimmerservice?
What is my room number?	Wie lautet meine Zimmernummer?
Here you have your room key.	Hier haben Sie Ihren Zimmerschlüssel.
Can I have more than one key?	Kann ich mehr als einen Schlüssel haben?
What is the Wi-Fi password?	Was ist das WLAN-Passwort?
Is breakfast included?	Ist das Frühstück inbegriffen?
I would like to get more towels.	Ich würde gerne mehr Handtücher bekommen.
I need more towels.	Ich brauche mehr Handtücher.
How often do you change the bedding?	Wie oft wechseln Sie die Bettwäsche?
I need to change the bedding, please.	Ich muss bitte die Bettwäsche wechseln.
How do I turn on the air conditioning?	Wie schalte ich die Klimaanlage ein?
How do I turn on the heating?	Wie schalte ich die Heizung ein?

How do I use the remote control for the AC?	Wie verwende ich die Fernbedienung für die Klimaanlage?
How do I use the remote control for the TV?	Wie verwende ich die Fernbedienung für den Fernseher?
The remote control needs batteries.	Die Fernbedienung benötigt Batterien.
Can you show me how to use the shower?	Können Sie mir zeigen, wie man die Dusche benutzt?
Can I keep the windows open?	Kann ich die Fenster offen lassen?
My room is too hot.	Mein Zimmer ist zu heiß.
My room is too cold.	Mein Zimmer ist zu kalt.
How do I use the telephone in my room?	Wie nutze ich das Telefon in meinem Zimmer?
Can I make domestic calls free of charge?	Kann ich Inlandsgespräche kostenlos führen?
What is the charge for international calls?	Wie hoch sind die Gebühren für Auslandsgespräche?
What is the desk number?	Wie lautet die Nummer für die Rezeption?
Is there a kitchen?	Gibt es eine Küche?
Is there a refrigerator?	Gibt es einen Kühlschrank?
Are there hangers in the closet?	Gibt es Kleiderbügel im Schrank?
Is there a hairdryer?	Gibt es einen Haartrockner?
Is there a mirror?	Gibt es einen Spiegel?
What are the breakfast hours?	Wie sind die Frühstückszeiten?
Breakfast service is from 7 a.m. to 10 a.m.	Der Frühstücksservice ist von 7.00 bis 10.00 Uhr verfügbar.
Where are restaurants nearby?	Wo sind Restaurants in der Nähe?
What public transportation options are available to major tourist attractions nearby?	Welche öffentlichen Verkehrsmittel stehen zu den wichtigsten Touristenattraktionen in der Nähe zur Verfügung?
How close is the bus station?	Wie nah ist der Busbahnhof?
How close is the metro station?	Wie nah ist die U-Bahn-Station?
How much is the bus fare?	Wie viel kostet der Bus?
How do I contact you in case of emergency?	Wie kann ich Sie im Notfall kontaktieren?
How do I get to the [destination] from this hotel?	Wie komme ich von diesem Hotel zum [Ziel]?
Where is the nearest ATM?	Wo ist der nächste Geldautomat?
Can I pay with cash?	Kann ich mit Bargeld bezahlen?
Do you accept credit cards?	Akzeptieren Sie Kreditkarten?
When does the swimming pool open?	Wann öffnet das Schwimmbad?

When does the restaurant open?	Wann öffnet das Restaurant?
When does the bar open?	Wann öffnet die Bar?
When does the museum open?	Wann öffnet das Museum?
How much is the parking fee?	Wie hoch ist die Parkgebühr?
Can I park in the area?	Kann ich in der Gegend parken?
Can I log into my streaming service accounts?	Kann ich mich bei meinen Streaming-Dienstkonten anmelden?
When is room cleaning done during my stay?	Wann erfolgt die Zimmerreinigung während meines Aufenthalts?
Is there a coffee machine in the room?	Gibt es eine Kaffeemaschine im Zimmer?
Can I have food from restaurants delivered to my room through room service?	Kann ich mir über den Zimmerservice Speisen aus Restaurants auf mein Zimmer liefern lassen?
Do you have tourist brochures?	Haben Sie Touristenbroschüren?
What guided tour do you recommend?	Welche Führung empfehlen Sie?
Where is the elevator?	Wo ist der Aufzug?
Where is the emergency exit?	Wo ist der Notausgang?
I do not need more towels.	Ich brauche keine weiteren Handtücher.
Can I smoke in the hotel?	Darf ich im Hotel rauchen?
Where are the designated smoking areas?	Wo sind die ausgewiesenen Raucherbereiche?
I would like to add more days to my reservation.	Ich möchte meiner Reservierung weitere Tage hinzufügen.
I would like to modify my reservation.	Ich möchte meine Reservierung ändern.
I'd like to make a dinner reservation.	Ich möchte ein Abendessen reservieren.
What are some places worth visiting in the area?	Welche Orte in der Umgebung sind einen Besuch wert?
Can you call me a taxi?	Können Sie mir ein Taxi rufen?
Do you work directly with a taxi company?	Arbeiten Sie direkt mit einem Taxiunternehmen zusammen?
Where is the largest shopping mall?	Wo ist das größte Einkaufszentrum?
What are the room amenities?	Welche Annehmlichkeiten gibt es im Zimmer?
Do you provide barbecue facilities?	Stellen Sie Grillmöglichkeiten zur Verfügung?
Do you have a conference room?	Haben Sie einen Konferenzraum?
How reliable is the Internet?	Wie zuverlässig ist das Internet?
How fast is the Internet?	Wie schnell ist das Internet?
Where are the good places for a stroll nearby?	Wo kann man in der Nähe gut spazieren gehen?

Does this hotel/Airbnb have activities for children?	Bietet dieses Hotel/Airbnb Aktivitäten für Kinder an?
Where are the art galleries or museums nearby?	Wo sind die Kunstgalerien oder Museen in der Nähe?
Is there a safe in the room?	Gibt es einen Safe im Zimmer?
What type of complementary breakfast do you offer?	Welche Art von kostenlosem Frühstück bieten Sie an?
Can I request a different breakfast if I want to?	Kann ich ein anderes Frühstück anfordern, wenn ich möchte?
What is the most famous restaurant in the city?	Welches ist das berühmteste Restaurant der Stadt?
What is the most famous museum in the city?	Welches ist das berühmteste Museum der Stadt?
Do you offer spa services?	Bieten Sie Wellnessangebote an?
Do you have a sauna?	Haben Sie eine Sauna?
What is the closest park?	Welcher Park ist am nächsten?
What is the closest café?	Welches ist das nächstgelegene Café?
Where is the closest Starbucks?	Wo ist der nächste Starbucks?
Is the city bike-friendly?	Ist die Stadt fahrradfreundlich?
Where can I rent a bike?	Wo kann ich ein Fahrrad mieten?
Where can I rent a scooter?	Wo kann ich einen Roller mieten?
Where can I rent a car?	Wo kann ich ein Auto mieten?
How do I get to the beach?	Wie komme ich zum Strand?
How do I get to the lake?	Wie komme ich zum See?
Does this hotel/Airbnb provide facilities for people with disabilities?	Bietet dieses Hotel/Airbnb Einrichtungen für Menschen mit Behinderungen?
Does this hotel/Airbnb offer ski equipment rental services?	Bietet dieses Hotel/Airbnb einen Skiausrüstungsverleih an?
Where is the golf course nearby?	Wo ist der Golfplatz in der Nähe?
Where is the souvenir shop?	Wo ist der Souvenirladen?
Do you have a souvenir shop in the hotel?	Haben Sie einen Souvenirladen im Hotel?
What is the price range for the souvenirs in the shops?	Wie hoch ist die Preisspanne für die Souvenirs in den Geschäften?
Where can I hire an airport shuttle?	Wo kann ich einen Flughafen-Shuttle mieten?
Do you offer a shuttle service?	Bieten Sie einen Shuttleservice an?
Is the airport shuttle service free?	Ist der Flughafentransfer kostenlos?
Where do locals go?	Wohin gehen Einheimische?
Where do locals eat?	Wo essen Einheimische?

What do locals do on the weekends?	Was machen Einheimische am Wochenende?
What is the snowboard equipment rental fee?	Wie hoch ist die Leihgebühr für die Snowboardausrüstung?
What is the surf equipment rental fee?	Wie hoch ist die Leihgebühr für die Surfausrüstung?
What is the outdoor equipment rental fee?	Wie hoch ist die Leihgebühr für Outdoor-Ausrüstung?
Where are the cultural centers or art spaces nearby?	Wo sind die Kulturzentren oder Kunsträume in der Nähe?
Does this hotel/Airbnb provide complementary water bottles?	Bietet dieses Hotel/Airbnb kostenlose Wasserflaschen an?

Vocabulary	Translation
Hotel	Hotel
Airbnb	Airbnb
Reservation	Reservierung
Check-in	Einchecken
Check-out	Auschecken
Room	Zimmer
Room number	Zimmernummer
Bed	Bett
Window	Fenster
Toilet	Toilette
Shower	Dusche
Sink	Waschbecken
Towel	Handtuch
Hand towel	Handtuch
Bathing robe	Bademantel
Fridge	Kühlschrank
Mini fridge	Minikühlschrank
Kitchen	Küche
Internet	Internet
Internet password	Internet-Passwort
Breakfast	Frühstück
Breakfast included	Frühstück inklusive
Breakfast time	Frühstückszeit
Room service	Zimmerservice
Parking	Parken

Parking included	Parkplatz inklusive
Parking fee	Parkgebühr
Lobby	Empfangshalle
Elevator	Aufzug
Smoking allowed area	Raucherbereich
Non-smoking area	Nichtraucherbereich
Pool	Schwimmbad
Gym	Fitnessstudio
Sauna	Sauna
Balcony	Balkon
TV	Fernseher
Remote control	Fernbedienung
Coffee machine	Kaffeemaschine
Bottled water	In Flaschen abgefülltes Wasser
Soap	Seife
Hand soap	Handseife
Shampoo	Shampoo
Conditioner	Spülung
Slippers	Hausschuhe
Credit card	Kreditkarte
Cash	Kasse
Sofa	Sofa
Safe	Safe
Bar	Bar
Playground	Spielplatz
Minibar	Minibar
Curtains	Vorhänge
Noise	Lärm
Noise-cancelling Windows	Fenster mit Geräuschunterdrückung
Hairdryer	Fön
Extra towels	Extra Handtücher
Restaurant	Restaurant
Desk number	Nummer der Rezeption
24-hour service	24-Stunden-Service

Chapter 4
Food, Restaurants, and Cafés

Food plays a significant role in German culture, with traditions such as Sunday lunches and hearty roasts bringing families together for communal dining experiences. Whether you're exploring local restaurants, traditional Gaststätten, or savoring street food, we're here to equip you with the language skills necessary to navigate the diverse world of German cuisine.

Throughout this chapter, we'll delve into a variety of topics related to food and dining in Germany. Here's a sneak peek at what lies ahead:

Foundations of Food Vocabulary: We'll provide you with a robust foundation of German food-related vocabulary, empowering you to identify ingredients, dishes, and flavors with ease.

Mastering the Art of Ordering: Whether you find yourself in a traditional German Gaststätte, a bustling market, or enjoying street food from a local vendor, you'll master the art of placing orders in German and confidently navigating menus.

Expressing Your Preferences: Discover how to confidently convey your food preferences, allergies, and dietary restrictions, ensuring that each meal caters to your tastes and requirements.

Asking Informed Questions: Equip yourself with the ability to ask questions about the menu, ingredients, and preparation methods, enabling you to make informed choices and engage in meaningful conversations with local chefs and fellow diners

By the time you reach the end of this chapter, you'll be well-prepared to savor the diverse and delectable dishes that Germany has to offer. You'll not only navigate the world of food and dining with ease but also engage in meaningful conversations with locals, forging connections through the universal language of cuisine. Together, we will build your conversational skills and explore the tantalizing world of German food! Guten Appetit!

Common Phrases	Translation
Can I have the menu, please?	Kann ich die Speisekarte haben?
Do you have free tables?	Haben Sie freie Tische?
Do you have tables by the windows/balcony?	Haben Sie Tische am Fenster/Balkon?
I am ready to order.	Ich bin bereit zu bestellen.
I'd like to order.	Ich möchte gerne bestellen.
Can we I have two more minutes? I'm not ready to order yet.	Können wir noch zwei Minuten haben? Ich bin noch nicht bereit zu bestellen.
What is the most popular dish?	Was ist das beliebteste Gericht?
What do you recommend?	Was empfehlen Sie?
What is this?	Was ist das?
Is this spicy?	Ist das scharf?
Can you make it spicier?	Können Sie es schärfer machen?

Can you make it less spicy?	Können Sie es weniger scharf machen?
I'll take this to go.	Ich nehme das mit.
Can I have a box/bag for this?	Kann ich dafür eine Box/Tasche haben?
Can I have the bill, please?	Kann ich bitte die Rechnung haben?
I'm ready to pay.	Ich bin bereit zu zahlen.
I'd like to pay.	Ich möchte zahlen.
Do you accept credit cards?	Akzeptieren Sie Kreditkarten?
Should I pay here at the table or at the cashier?	Soll ich hier am Tisch oder an der Kasse bezahlen?
We only accept cash.	Wir akzeptieren nur Bargeld.
Tips are included in the bill.	Trinkgelder sind in der Rechnung enthalten.
Tips are voluntary.	Trinkgelder sind freiwillig.
The food here is good.	Das Essen hier ist gut.
The meal was delicious.	Das Essen war köstlich.
I'm vegetarian.	Ich bin Vegetarier.
I'm vegan.	Ich bin Veganer.
I don't eat meat.	Ich esse kein Fleisch.
I have allergies to…	Ich habe Allergien gegen …
I'd like to drink…	Ich würde gerne... trinken.
I would like to have some water.	Ich hätte gerne etwas Wasser.
I'd like a cup of wine…	Ich hätte gerne ein Glas Wein …
To drink, I want a carbonated water.	Zum Trinken möchte ich ein Mineralwasser.
Can I have cold water?	Kann ich kaltes Wasser haben?
One bottle of water, please.	Eine Flasche Wasser, bitte.
It smells good.	Es riecht gut.
Please, I need some extra sauce.	Bitte, ich brauche etwas mehr Soße.
Can you pass me the salt?	Können Sie mir das Salz geben?
Can you pass me the pepper?	Können Sie mir den Pfeffer reichen?
What is the most popular dish?	Was ist das beliebteste Gericht?
I'd like to have a coffee.	Ich möchte einen Kaffee trinken.
I'd like to have an espresso.	Ich hätte gerne einen Espresso.
I'd like to have an Americano.	Ich hätte gerne einen Americano.
How much is this?	Wieviel kostet das?
What time do you close?	Um wie viel Uhr machen Sie zu?
What time do you open?	Um wie viel Uhr öffnen Sie?
I want to order some dessert.	Ich möchte etwas Nachtisch bestellen.
Can I have an extra spoon?	Kann ich einen zusätzlichen Löffel haben?

Can I have an extra fork?	Kann ich eine zusätzliche Gabel haben?
Can I have an extra plate?	Kann ich einen zusätzlichen Teller haben?
Can I have more napkins?	Kann ich mehr Servietten haben?
I'm sorry.	Es tut mir Leid.
Thank you so much!	Vielen Dank!
Can you repeat that, please?	Können Sie das bitte wiederholen?
The food is to go.	Das Essen ist zum Mitnehmen.
I would like to make a reservation.	Ich würde gerne etwas reservieren.
Please, pack this to go.	Bitte packen Sie das für unterwegs ein.
Do you need anything else?	Brauchen Sie noch was?
Would you like to order anything else?	Möchten Sie noch etwas bestellen?
When will the food be ready?	Wann ist das Essen fertig?
You will have to wait a little longer than usual.	Sie müssen etwas länger als gewöhnlich warten.
How is this dish prepared?	Wie wird dieses Gericht zubereitet?
Does it contain…?	Enthält es…?
White rice, please!	Weißer Reis, bitte!
I want scrambled eggs.	Ich möchte Rührei.
I want scrambled eggs with ham.	Ich möchte Rührei mit Schinken.
I want sunny-side eggs.	Ich möchte Spiegeleier von beiden Seiten gebraten.
It is my first time trying this kind of food.	Es ist das erste Mal, dass ich diese Art von Essen probiere.
I'm loving it!	Ich liebe es!
What types of bread do you have?	Welche Brotsorten gibt es bei Ihnen?
Does it contain caffeine?	Enthält es Koffein?
I would like to try some street food.	Ich würde gerne etwas Streetfood probieren.
Where can I order pizza?	Wo kann ich Pizza bestellen?
What are the healthy options?	Welche gesunden Optionen gibt es?
I'd like to order a sweet dessert.	Ich möchte ein süßes Dessert bestellen.
I can't eat dairy products.	Ich kann keine Milchprodukte essen.
Can I have a salad, please?	Kann ich bitte einen Salat haben?
Do you have a kids' menu?	Gibt es ein Kindermenü?
Please, add more cheese.	Bitte geben Sie mehr Käse hinzu.
Do you have a buffet?	Haben Sie ein Buffet?
Are the drinks unlimited?	Sind die Getränke unbegrenzt?
I would like to add something to my order…	Ich möchte meiner Bestellung etwas hinzufügen…

Where is the bathroom?	Wo ist die Toilette?
Where can I pay?	Wo kann ich bezahlen?
The place is beautiful.	Der Ort ist wunderschön.
I'll leave a positive review!	Ich hinterlasse eine positive Bewertung!
I'd definitively come back!	Ich würde auf jeden Fall wiederkommen!
I'd love the service!	Ich würde den Service lieben!

Common Vocabulary	Translation
Food	Essen
Breakfast	Frühstück
Lunch	Mittagessen
Dinner	Abendessen
Snack	Snack
Meat	Fleisch
Chicken	Huhn
Beef	Rindfleisch
Pork	Schweinefleisch
Fish	Fisch
Vegetables	Gemüse
Onion	Zwiebel
Carrot	Karotte
Mushroom	Pilz
Pepper	Pfeffer
Jalapeno	Jalapeno
Lettuce	Kopfsalat
Cabbage	Kohl
Tomato	Tomate
Tomato sauce	Tomatensauce
Milk	Milch
Cheese	Käse
Cream	Creme/Sahne
Butter	Butter
Egg	Ei
Bread	Brot
Fruit	Obst
Apple	Apfel
Banana	Banane

Pear	Birne
Watermelon	Wassermelone
Melon	Melone
Pineapple	Ananas
Strawberry	Erdbeere
Beans	Bohnen
Rice	Reis
Pasta	Pasta
Salt	Salz
Pepper	Pfeffer
Sugar	Zucker
Oil	Öl
Vinegar	Essig
Garlic	Knoblauch
Spices	Gewürze
Seasoning	Gewürze
Dressing	Dressing
Salad	Salat
Menu	Speisekarte
Restaurant	Restaurant
Café	Cafe
Bakery	Bäckerei
Butchery	Metzgerei
Soup	Suppe
Appetizer	Vorspeise
Main Dish	Hauptgericht
Dessert	Nachtisch
Wine	Wein
Water	Wasser
Carbonated water	Mineralwasser
Cider	Apfelwein
Grilled	Gegrillt
Baked	Gebacken
Steamed	Gedämpft
Well-done	Durch
Half-done	Medium
Stew	Eintopf

Sushi	Sushi
Sandwich	Sandwich
Ham	Schinken
Toast	Toast
Spoon	Löffel
Fork	Gabel
Knife	Messer
Plate	Tisch
Cup	Tasse
Napkin	Serviette
Glass	Glas
Cutlery	Besteck
Kitchen	Küche
Ice cream	Eiscreme
Cake	Kuchen
Hamburger	Hamburger
Typical food	Typisches Essen
Street food	Streetfood
Bacon	Speck/Bacon

Chapter 5
The Shopping Experience in German-Speaking Countries

In both Germany and German-speaking regions, shopping transcends the act of mere transactions; it's a cultural odyssey waiting to be explored. Trust us, you have never experienced shopping as you will in a German-speaking country. Whether you're a fashion enthusiast tracking the latest trends or a collector in search of unique treasures, there's an adventure tailored to everyone's tastes.

From navigating the bustling traditional markets of Berlin, Munich, or Vienna, to exploring the charming boutiques of Hamburg, Zurich, or Cologne, or wandering through the modern shopping malls of Frankfurt or Bern, this chapter aims to empower you to interact confidently with locals and shopkeepers alike. With a diverse array of shopping experiences, spanning the historic markets of Nuremberg to the vibrant artisan markets of Heidelberg, you'll learn the nuances of greeting and engaging with shopkeepers and fellow shoppers.

Discover how to inquire about product details, sizes, and prices, adeptly negotiate and bargain, express your preferences with cultural finesse, make informed purchasing decisions, seek guidance in sprawling shopping centers, and grasp the essential vocabulary for various shopping scenarios.

Whether you're on the hunt for the latest fashion trends, traditional crafts from Germany or other German-speaking regions, or simply looking to immerse yourself in the dynamic market cultures, our guide is designed to empower you to make the most of your shopping experiences across the German-speaking regions, combining the rich tapestry of Germany and the diverse flavors of German-speaking cultures.

Common Phrases	Translation
How much is it?	Wie viel kostet das?
What is the price?	Was ist der Preis?
Does it have a discount?	Gibt es einen Rabatt?
Can you give me a discount?	Können Sie mir einen Rabatt geben?
Do you have this in a different color?	Haben Sie das in einer anderen Farbe?
Do you have this in a different size?	Gibt es das in einer anderen Größe?
Can I pay with cash?	Kann ich mit Bargeld bezahlen?
Can I pay with credit card?	Kann ich mit Kreditkarte zahlen?
Can I pay with my credit card point?	Kann ich mit meiner Kreditkarte bezahlen?
Can I pay with my credit card miles?	Kann ich mit meinen Kreditkartenmeilen bezahlen?
Do you offer loyalty reward points?	Bieten Sie Treueprämienpunkte an?
Here you have your receipt.	Hier haben Sie Ihre Quittung.
Here you have your product.	Hier haben Sie Ihr Produkt.
Do you need a bag?	Brauchen Sie eine Tüte?
Is this the final price?	Ist das der Endpreis?
Does the price include taxes?	Sind im Preis Steuern enthalten?

The price does not include taxes.	Der Preis beinhaltet keine Steuern.
Is there a discount for bulk purchases?	Gibt es einen Rabatt für Großeinkäufe?
I need a receipt, please.	Ich brauche bitte eine Quittung.
Can I try it?	Kann ich es probieren?
Can I try in on?	Kann ich es anprobieren?
Where is the fitting room?	Wo ist die Umkleidekabine?
Do you have this in a bigger size?	Gibt es das in einer größeren Größe?
Do you have this in a smaller size?	Gibt es das auch in einer kleineren Größe?
Do you accept returns?	Akzeptieren Sie Rücksendungen?
What is the return policy?	Wie lauten die Rückgabebedingungen?
We do not accept returns.	Wir akzeptieren keine Rücksendungen.
We accept returns if the product still has the tags.	Wir akzeptieren Rücksendungen, wenn das Produkt noch mit den Etiketten versehen ist.
How long is the sale going on?	Wie lange geht der Schlussverkauf?
How long will the discount last?	Wie lange gilt der Rabatt?
What is the most popular brand?	Was ist die beliebteste Marke?
What is the most popular product?	Was ist das beliebteste Produkt?
What material is it made of?	Aus welchem Material besteht er?
It is made of synthetic material.	Es besteht aus synthetischem Material.
It is made of leather.	Es besteht aus Leder.
It is made of denim.	Es ist aus Jeans gefertigt.
I like this handbag.	Ich mag diese Handtasche.
I like those shoes.	Ich mag diese Schuhe.
I don't like the wallet.	Mir gefällt das Portemonnaie nicht.
I don't like these pants.	Ich mag diese Hose nicht.
Does the product have warranty?	Hat das Produkt eine Garantie?
How long does the warranty last?	Wie lange dauert die Garantie?
Can I see it?	Kann ich es sehen?
Can you show that product over there?	Können Sie das Produkt dort zeigen?
You can see it.	Sie können es sehen.
You can try it.	Sie können es probieren.
It is not for sale.	Es steht nicht zum Verkauf.
Is it for sale?	Steht es zum Verkauf?
What is the lowest price?	Was ist der niedrigste Preis?
What is the best price you can offer?	Was ist der beste Preis, den Sie anbieten können?

Can I find this product in other stores?	Kann ich dieses Produkt in anderen Geschäften finden?
It is an exclusive product.	Es handelt sich um ein exklusives Produkt.
It is not available in other stores.	Es ist nicht in anderen Geschäften erhältlich.
This is a perfect gift.	Dies ist ein perfektes Geschenk.
It is a unique gift.	Es ist ein einzigartiges Geschenk.
What do you recommend?	Was empfehlen Sie?
What time does the shop open?	Um wie viel Uhr öffnet der Laden?
What time does the shop close?	Um wie viel Uhr schließt der Laden?
Is it open during the weekends?	Ist es am Wochenende geöffnet?
This is the best price.	Das ist der beste Preis.
It is a reasonable price.	Es ist ein angemessener Preis.
You will not find a better price.	Sie werden keinen besseren Preis finden.
It is really beautiful.	Es ist wirklich wunderschön.
It is really special.	Es ist wirklich etwas Besonderes.
It represents our culture.	Es repräsentiert unsere Kultur.
It is a traditional dress.	Es ist ein traditionelles Kleid.
It is a traditional hat.	Es ist ein traditioneller Hut.
Can you ship it to my country?	Können Sie es in mein Land versenden?
How much is the shipping to my country?	Wie viel kostet der Versand in mein Land?
What is the weight of this?	Wie schwer ist das?
Where is this made?	Wo wird das hergestellt?
How do I have to take care of it?	Wie pflege ich es?
Can I see it first?	Kann ich es zuerst sehen?
Can I open the package?	Kann ich das Paket öffnen?
You cannot open the package, but I have a product sample.	Sie können das Paket nicht öffnen, aber ich habe ein Produktmuster.
What type of sounds does it make?	Welche Art von Geräuschen macht es?
Does it have special features?	Hat es Besonderheiten?
Is this a new product?	Ist das ein neues Produkt?
Can you wrap it as a present?	Kann man es als Geschenk verpacken?
Does it have an additional cost?	Ist es mit zusätzlichen Kosten verbunden?
I can wrap it as a present with no additional cost.	Ich kann es ohne zusätzliche Kosten als Geschenk verpacken.
Do you accept discount coupons?	Akzeptieren Sie Rabattgutscheine?
Can I have a better price if I buy more than one?	Kann ich einen besseren Preis erzielen, wenn ich mehr als eins kaufe?
How long does the shipping take?	Wie lange dauert der Versand?

Is it available online?	Ist es online verfügbar?
Is it sold on the Internet?	Wird es im Internet verkauft?
Is it safe for kids?	Ist es sicher für Kinder?
The product is for 3-year-old kids or older.	Das Produkt ist für Kinder ab 3 Jahren geeignet.
The product is not safe for kids.	Das Produkt ist für Kinder nicht sicher.
It is not a safe product for carry-on luggage.	Es handelt sich nicht um ein sicheres Produkt für Handgepäck.
Is there any type of allergic reaction?	Gibt es irgendeine Art von allergischer Reaktion?
What type of warranty does the product have?	Welche Art von Garantie hat das Produkt?
What type of warranty do you offer?	Welche Art von Garantie bieten Sie an?
Can it be customized?	Kann es angepasst werden?
Can my name be engraved?	Kann mein Name eingraviert werden?
What is the return policy?	Wie lauten die Rückgabebedingungen?
Can I pay with dollars?	Kann ich mit Dollar bezahlen?
Can I pay with the local currency?	Kann ich mit der Landeswährung bezahlen?
Are taxes included?	Sind Steuern inbegriffen?
Is this the final price?	Ist das der Endpreis?
The best store in the city is…	Der beste Laden der Stadt ist…
The best shopping mall in the city is…	Das beste Einkaufszentrum der Stadt ist…
How do you use it?	Wie benutzt man es?
How do you eat it?	Wie isst man es?
The telephone price is…	Der Telefonpreis beträgt…
The book price is…	Der Buchpreis beträgt…
It has special features.	Es verfügt über Besonderheiten.
It is a traditional product.	Es ist ein traditionelles Produkt.
This is the best store in the country.	Das ist der beste Laden im Land.
This is the most exclusive product we have.	Dies ist das exklusivste Produkt, das wir haben.
Add it to my bill.	Fügen Sie es meiner Rechnung hinzu.
I won't buy it.	Ich werde es nicht kaufen.
I don't need it.	Ich brauche es nicht.
I'll pick it up tomorrow.	Ich hole es morgen ab.

Common Vocabulary	Translation
Shopping	Einkaufen
Store	Speichern

Shopping mall	Einkaufszentrum
Market	Markt
Open-air market	Freiluftmarkt
Supermarket	Supermarkt
Product	Produkt
Price	Preis
Package	Paket
Box	Kiste
Tag	Etikett
Sell	Verkaufen
Transaction	Transaktion
Payment	Zahlung
Pay with cash	Bezahle mit Bargeld
Pay with card	Bezahlen mit Karte
Receipt	Quittung
Reimbursement	Erstattung
Warranty	Garantie
Size	Größe
Color	Farbe
Shape	Form
Brand	Marke
Style	Stil
Origin	Herkunft
Model	Modell
Manufacturing date	Herstellungsdatum
Manufacturing place	Herstellungsort
Expiration date	Verfallsdatum
To try something on	etwas anzuprobieren
Features	Merkmale
Special features	Besondere Merkmale
Material	Material
Fabric	Stoff
Denim	Jeans
Polyester	Polyester
Synthetic	Synthetik
Leather	Leder
Wool	Wolle

Seller	Verkäufer
Consumer	Verbraucher/Kunde
Event	Ereignis
Coupon	Coupon
Discount coupon	Rabattgutschein
Deposit	Kaution
Installment	Rate
Interest-free installment	Zinslose Rate
Exchange	Austausch
Quality	Qualität
Quantity	Menge
Variety	Vielfalt
Unbox	Auspacken
Exchange rate	Wechselkurs
Local currency	Landeswährung
Dollars	Dollar
Euros	Euro
Wholesale discount	Großhandelsrabatt
Unit discount	Einheitenrabatt
Shop owner	Ladenbesitzer
Credit card points	Kreditkartenpunkte
Credit card miles	Kreditkartenmeilen
Loyalty points	Treuepunkte
Return	Zurück geben
Return policy	Rückgaberecht
Defect	Defekt
Sleeve	Ärmel
Long sleeve	Lange Ärmel
Short sleeve	Kurzarm
Sleeveless	Ärmellos
Shopping kart	Einkaufswagen
ATM	Geldautomat
Watch	Betrachten
Wristwatch	Armbanduhr
Bracelet	Armband
Shoe	Schuh
Sole	Sohle

Shoelace	Schnürsenkel
High heel	High Heels
Sandal / Flip flops	Sandale / Flip-Flops
Ring	Ring
Earrings	Ohrringe
Hat	Hut
Beach hat	Strandhut
Bag	Tasche
Scarf	Schal
Sweater	Pullover
Coat	Mantel
Wallet	Geldbörse
Purse	Handtasche
Shirt	Hemd
T-shirt	T-Shirt
Skirt	Rock
Dress	Kleid
Pants	Hose
Suit	Anzug
Belt	Gürtel
Formal shoes	Formale Schuhe
Sneakers	Turnschuhe
Swimsuit	Badeanzug
Lingerie	Unterwäsche
Underwear	Unterwäsche
Baseball cap	Baseball Kappe
Headphones	Kopfhörer
Speaker	Lautsprecher
Phone	Telefon
Computer	Computer
Laptop	Laptop
Book	Buch
Bestseller	Bestseller
Inventory	Inventar
Customer satisfaction	Kundenzufriedenheit
Review	Rezension
Product review	Produktbewertung

Store review	Laden-Rezension
Order number	Bestellnummer
Date of delivery	Lieferdatum
Receipt verification	Empfangsbestätigung
Cashier	Kassierer
Free sale	Freiverkauf
Value for money	Preis-Leistungs-Verhältnis
Seasonal sale	Saisonverkauf
Brand logo	Markenlogo
Price comparison	Preisvergleich
Fitting room	Umkleidekabine
Manager	Manager
Sale advisor	Verkaufsberater
Consumer protection	Verbraucherschutz
Price adjustment	Preisanpassung
Free trial	Kostenlose Testphase
Offer	Angebot
On sale	Im Angebot
Advertisement	Werbung
Reward program	Belohnungsprogramm
Order confirmation	Bestellbestätigung
Withdrawal	Rückzug
Money withdrawal	Geldabhebung
Window-shop	Schaufensterbummel

Chapter 6
Drugstores and Hospital Visits in German-Speaking Countries

Germany and German-speaking regions are renowned for their rich history, diverse cuisine, and stunning landscapes. There is also a thriving drinking culture that plays a significant role in the social fabric of the nation. People in these regions are known for their strong sense of community and the tendency to form connections over shared meals or rounds of drinks. Whether it's enjoying a glass of wine, savoring local beer, or indulging in beloved traditional dishes, these communal gatherings provide opportunities for connection, celebration, and relaxation from the demands of daily life. However, a night of merriment can sometimes lead to a challenging experience, especially for visitors who are not aware of various remedies and cures available.

Other emergencies are also possible. Navigating a hospital or pharmacy in a foreign country can be a daunting task, especially when you're not feeling well. With these questions and phrases, you will gain the confidence to express your needs, symptoms, and concerns effectively in German, ensuring a positive experience during medical visits.

We want to emphasize this: we hope you never need these phrases for yourself, and that your trip to any German-speaking country is full of wonderful experiences. However, we are aware that sometimes not everything goes as planned – you might feel unwell, have an accident, or even find yourself in unexpected situations. If something like this happens, we've got you covered with all the phrases and vocabulary that you will learn in this chapter.

Common Phrases	Translation
I need help.	Ich brauche Hilfe.
I need medical help.	Ich brauche medizinische Hilfe.
I need to see a doctor.	Ich muss einen Arzt aufsuchen.
I need to go to a hospital.	Ich muss in ein Krankenhaus.
Please, call a doctor.	Bitte rufen Sie einen Arzt.
Please, take me to an emergency room.	Bitte bringen Sie mich in eine Notaufnahme.
I have so much pain.	Ich habe so große Schmerzen.
I have fever.	Ich habe Fieber.
I have a headache.	Ich habe Kopfschmerzen.
I have a back pain.	Ich habe Rückenschmerzen.
My feet hurt.	Meine Füße tun weh.
I have a stomachache.	Ich habe Bauchschmerzen.
My belly hurts.	Ich habe Bauchweh.
I have cramps.	Ich habe Krämpfe.
I broke my arm.	Ich habe meinen Arm gebrochen.
I broke my shoulder.	Ich habe mir die Schulter gebrochen.
I broke my leg.	Ich habe mir das Bein gebrochen.
I need to vomit.	Ich muss mich übergeben.
I have nauseas.	Ich habe Übelkeit.

I feel dizzy.	Mir ist schwindlig.
I am going to throw up.	Ich muss mich übergeben.
I have diarrhea.	Ich habe Durchfall.
I am dehydrated.	Ich bin dehydriert.
I have a running nose.	Ich habe eine laufende Nase.
I have an allergy.	Ich habe eine Allergie.
I have a cold.	Ich habe eine Erkältung.
I'm in too much pain to move.	Ich habe zu große Schmerzen, um mich zu bewegen.
I have diabetes.	Ich habe Diabetes.
My sugar level is high.	Mein Zuckerspiegel ist hoch.
My sugar level is low.	Mein Zuckerspiegel ist niedrig.
My blood pressure is high.	Mein Blutdruck ist hoch.
My blood pressure is low.	Mein Blutdruck ist niedrig.
I feel weak.	Ich fühle mich schwach.
I am sick.	Ich bin krank.
I am bleeding.	Ich blute.
I need a thermometer.	Ich brauche ein Thermometer.
Can you give me a prescription?	Können Sie mir ein Rezept geben?
I need medication for…	Ich brauche Medikamente für …
What is the recommended dose?	Was ist die empfohlene Dosis?
You need to take this pill after eating.	Sie müssen diese Pille nach dem Essen einnehmen.
You need to take this pill before eating.	Sie müssen diese Pille vor dem Essen einnehmen.
You need to take this test before having breakfast.	Sie müssen diesen Test vor dem Frühstück machen.
You need to take this test after having breakfast.	Sie müssen diesen Test nach dem Frühstück machen.
I am allergic to…	Ich bin allergisch gegen…
I have allergies to…	Ich habe Allergien gegen …
I need a pill to sleep.	Ich brauche eine Pille zum Schlafen.
Where can I buy this medication?	Wo kann ich dieses Medikament kaufen?
I have a horrible hangover.	Ich habe einen schrecklichen Kater.
I need to drink electrolytes.	Ich muss Elektrolyte trinken.
I need a glass of water.	Ich brauche ein Glas Wasser.
I need dan energy drink.	Ich brauche einen Energydrink.
The patient needs to rest.	Der Patient muss sich ausruhen.

You need to rest.	Sie müssen sich ausruhen.
I need to sleep.	Ich muss schlafen.
I feel weak. I need to sit.	Ich fühle mich schwach. Ich muss sitzen.
What is the treatment?	Was ist die Behandlung?
What is the treatment price?	Wie hoch ist der Behandlungspreis?
How long should I take the treatment?	Wie lange sollte ich die Behandlung durchführen?
What is the recovery period?	Was ist die Erholungsphase?
The recovery is fast.	Die Erholung erfolgt schnell.
The recovery is generally slow.	Die Erholung verläuft im Allgemeinen langsam.
Do I need to register as a patient?	Muss ich mich als Patient registrieren?
Where is the hospital?	Wo ist das Krankenhaus?
Where is the clinic?	Wo ist die Klinik?
Where is the drugstore?	Wo ist die Drogerie?
You need to wait for the doctor.	Sie müssen auf den Arzt warten.
The nurse Will take your information.	Die Krankenschwester wird Ihre Daten entgegennehmen.
I need to be hospitalized.	Ich muss ins Krankenhaus eingeliefert werden.
This is my information.	Das sind meine Informationen.
These are my documents.	Das sind meine Dokumente.
The information of my medical insurance is here.	Die Informationen meiner Krankenversicherung finden Sie hier.
I don't have a medical insurance.	Ich habe keine Krankenversicherung.
I have a medical insurance.	Ich habe eine Krankenversicherung.
I need a blood test.	Ich brauche eine Blutuntersuchung.
Can I buy this medication without a prescription?	Kann ich dieses Medikament ohne Rezept kaufen?
You can't do exercise for a month.	Sie können einen Monat lang keinen Sport treiben.
You can't eat greasy food for a month.	Sie können einen Monat lang kein fettiges Essen zu sich nehmen.
You can't consume alcoholic drinks for a month.	Einen Monat lang dürfen Sie keine alkoholischen Getränke konsumieren.
You can't make any physical effort for a month.	Sie können einen Monat lang keine körperliche Anstrengung unternehmen.
I need to go to a dentist.	Ich muss zum Zahnarzt gehen.
It is uncomfortable.	Es ist unangenehm.

It is a severe pain.	Es ist ein starker Schmerz.
I am not sick. I have a hangover.	Ich bin nicht krank. Ich habe einen Kater.
Where can I see my medical records?	Wo kann ich meine Krankenakten einsehen?
When Will I get the results?	Wann erhalte ich die Ergebnisse?
What is the diagnosis?	Wie lautet die Diagnose?
I have itching.	Ich habe Juckreiz.
Where can I buy a thermometer?	Wo kann ich ein Thermometer kaufen?
Where can I buy an oximeter?	Wo kann ich ein Oximeter kaufen?
I can't breathe.	Ich kann nicht atmen.
Please, call an ambulance.	Bitte rufen Sie einen Krankenwagen.
How do you feel?	Wie fühlen Sie sich?
I feel…	Ich fühle…
How did the accident happen?	Wie ist der Unfall passiert?
Where did the accident happen?	Wo ist der Unfall passiert?
What happened after?	Was geschah danach?
Does your head hurt?	Tut Ihr Kopf weh?
Does your body hurt?	Tut Ihr Körper weh?
Do you have or have you had fever?	Haben oder hatten Sie Fieber?
Can you give me an ID card?	Können Sie mir einen Ausweis geben?
I fell down the stairs.	Ich fiel die Treppe hinunter.
I sprained my ankle.	Ich habe mir den Fuß verstaucht.
I need a wheelchair.	Ich brauche einen Rollstuhl.
I think I broke my arm.	Ich glaube, ich habe mir den Arm gebrochen.
I broke my leg.	Ich brach mein Bein.
I have symptoms of food poisoning.	Ich habe Symptome einer Lebensmittelvergiftung.
My eyes are red.	Meine Augen sind rot.
I have a throat infection.	Ich habe eine Halsentzündung.
I have a urinary tract infection.	Ich habe eine Harnwegsinfektion.
The remedy is not working.	Das Mittel wirkt nicht.
You need a surgery.	Sie brauchen eine Operation.
You need to go back to your country.	Sie müssen in Ihr Land zurückkehren.
When is your return flight?	Wann ist Ihr Rückflug?
In this condition, you can't fly.	In diesem Zustand können Sie nicht fliegen.
What is your emergency contact information?	Wie lauten Ihre Notfallkontaktinformationen?
Don't worry!	Mach dir keine Sorgen!
Everything will be alright.	Alles wird gut werden.

Common Vocabulary	Translation
Doctor	Arzt
Nurse	Krankenschwester
Hospital	Krankenhaus
Clinic	Klinik
Emergency	Notfall
Emergency room	Notaufnahme
Patient	Patient
Ambulance	Krankenwagen
Medical test	Medizinischer Test
Test	Test
Medication	Medikamente
Pill	Pille
Syrup	Sirup
Injection	Spritze
Vaccine	Impfstoff
Consultation	Beratung
Hospital room	Krankenhauszimmer
Drugstore	Drogerie
Diagnosis	Diagnose
Painkiller	Schmerzmittel
Rash	Ausschlag
Sleeping pill	Schlaftablette
Thermometer	Thermometer
Blood pressure	Blutdruck
Blood pressure monitor	Blutdruckmonitor
Vitamin	Vitamin
Type	Typ
Dose	Dosis
Side effects	Nebenwirkungen
How to take it	Wie man es einnimmt
After eating	Nach dem Essen
Before eating	Vor dem Essen
After the shower	Nach dem Duschen
Before the shower	Vor der Dusche
Expiration date	Verfallsdatum
Warning	Warnung

Oximeter	Oximeter
Storage instructions	Aufbewahrungshinweise
Hangover	Kater
Hangover remedy	Mittel gegen Kater
Water	Wasser
Dehydration	Dehydrierung
Dehydrated	Dehydriert
Pain	Schmerz
Headache	Kopfschmerzen
Body ache	Körperschmerzen
Pain in the back	Rückenschmerzen
Pain in the neck	Nackenschmerzen
Stomachache	Magenschmerzen
Bellyache	Bauchschmerzen
Pain in the feet	Schmerzen in den Füßen
Pain in the hands	Schmerzen in den Händen
Food poisoning	Lebensmittelvergiftung
Vomit	Sich erbrechen
Diarrhea	Durchfall
Intoxication/poisoning	Vergiftung
Treatment	Behandlung
To be in pain	Schmerzen haben
Recovery	Erholung
X-rays	Röntgenstrahlen
Tomography	Tomographie
Medical record	Krankenakte
Anesthesia	Anästhesie
Surgery	Operation
Surgeon	Der Chirurg
Medical insurance	Krankenversicherung
Insurance bill	Versicherungsrechnung
Medical staff	Medizinische Angestellte
Medical assessment	Medizinische Beurteilung
Fracture	Fraktur
Broken arm	Gebrochener Arm
Broken leg	Gebrochenes Bein
Wheelchair	Rollstuhl

Burn	Brennen
Wound	Wunde
Accident	Unfall
Traffic accident	Verkehrsunfall
Fall	Fallen
Reaction	Reaktion
Allergic reaction	Allergische Reaktion
Treatment reaction	Behandlungsreaktion
General doctor	Allgemeinarzt
Obstetrician/ Gynecologist	Geburtshelfer/Gynäkologe
Dentist	Zahnarzt
Blood type	Blutgruppe
Infection	Infektion
Effect	Wirkung
Medicinal effect	Medizinische Wirkung
COVID test	COVID-Test
Pregnancy test	Schwangerschaftstest
STD	Geschlechtskrankheit
Liquid	Flüssig
Doctor prescription	Rezept vom Arzt
Syringe	Spritze
Diet	Diät
Supplementary diet	Beikost
Electrolytes	Elektrolyte
Adverse reaction	Nebenwirkung
Medication abuse	Medikamentenmissbrauch
Alcohol addiction	Alkoholabhängigkeit
Symptoms	Symptome
Hangover symptoms	Kater-Symptome
Symptoms of intoxication	Vergiftungssymptome
Symptoms of food poisoning	Symptome einer Lebensmittelvergiftung
Detox drink	Detox-Getränk
Dizziness	Schwindel
Nauseas	Übelkeit
Prevention	Verhütung
Gloves	Handschuhe
Vomit bag	Spucktüte

Remedy	Abhilfe
Alcohol	Alkohol
Shoulder	Schulter
Ankle	Knöchel
Eyes	Augen
Sleep	Schlafen
Treatment plan	Behandlungsplan
Hospital bill	Krankenhausrechnung
Covered by the insurance	Von der Versicherung abgedeckt
Blood	Blut
Blood tests	Bluttests
Patient information	Informationen zum Patienten
See a doctor	Einen Arzt aufsuchen
Consult with a doctor	Konsultieren Sie einen Arzt

Chapter 7
What to avoid doing in Germany

Navigating cultural norms in Germany requires a deep understanding of social etiquette. Punctuality is a cornerstone of German culture, and arriving late without a valid reason can be perceived as disrespectful. Germans highly value structured communication, so interrupting others while they are speaking is generally considered impolite. Engaging in conversations with a measured and moderate tone is appreciated, and speaking loudly, especially in public places, may be seen as disruptive.

Greetings play a crucial role in German social interactions. When entering a room or joining a group, it's customary to offer a polite greeting. Failure to do so might be considered impolite. Additionally, Germans often prefer the use of titles and formal address, especially in more formal settings. It's advisable to use titles and the formal "Sie" address until you are invited to switch to a more casual tone.

Germany is known for its strict recycling rules, so it's important to familiarize yourself with the local waste separation system to dispose of trash correctly. In terms of attire, Germans generally dress conservatively, especially in professional or business settings. It's wise to avoid overly casual or revealing clothing in these environments.

Given Germany's history, discussions about World War II and the Nazi era should be approached with sensitivity. Jokes or casual remarks about these topics are generally inappropriate. Public displays of affection may also be viewed conservatively in certain areas, so it's advisable to keep romantic gestures private.

When participating in a group toast, it's customary to make eye contact, say "Prost" (cheers), and clink glasses before taking a sip. Failing to do so may be considered impolite.

While these guidelines provide a general overview, it's important to recognize that cultural norms can vary, and individuals may have different preferences. Adapting to local customs and observing social cues will contribute to a smoother and more respectful experience in Germany.

Common Vocabulary	Translation
punctuality	Pünktlichkeit
Punctual	Rechtzeitig/pünktlich
Tardiness	Verspätung
Interrupt	Unterbrechen
Moderate tone	Moderater Ton
Speaking loudly	Lautes Sprechen
Polite	Höflich
Gift	Geschenk
Wrapping paper	Geschenkpapier
Thank you card	Dankeskarte

Gifting	Schenken
Guest gift	Gastgeschenk
Good day	Guten Tag
Good morning	Guten Morgen
Good evening	Guten Abend
Waste separation	Mülltrennung
Recycling rules	Recyclingregeln
Garbage disposal	Müllentsorgung
Clothing	Kleidung
Gala	Gala
Suit	Anzug
evening dress	Abendkleid
Invitation	Einladung
Reception	Empfang
Business clothing	Business-Kleidung
Casual	Casual
Revealing clothing	Enthüllende Kleidung
Sensitive topics	Sensible Themen
History	Geschichte
Second World War	Zweiter Weltkrieg
National Socialism	Nationalsozialismus
Public display of affection	Öffentliche Zärtlichkeiten
Reserved	Zurückhaltend
Romantic gestures	Romantische Gesten
Personal space	Persönlicher Raum
keep distance	Abstand halten
Considerate	Rücksichtsvoll
To be pushy	Aufdringlich sein
Private	Privat
To toast	Anstoßen
Cheers	Prost
Eye contact	Blickkontakt
Raise a glass	Glas erheben
Cultural adaptation	Kulturelle Anpassung
Social norms	Soziale Normen
Local customs	Lokale Bräuche
Adaptable	Anpassungsfähig

observation	Beobachtung
business lunch	Geschäftsessen
Business card	Visitenkarte
Business partner	Geschäftspartner
Professionalism	Seriosität
negotiation	Verhandlung

Conclusion

In conclusion, we are confident that this conversational German book has been a journey of language discovery and cultural exploration. As we've navigated through various dialogues and situations you'll likely encounter during your travels, you have not only refined your German conversational skills but also gained a deeper understanding of the diverse tapestry of German culture.

From casual chit-chat to more profound discussions, this book has equipped you with a diverse range of conversational scenarios, and we can be sure that you are ready to engage in real-life German conversations. The emphasis on practical vocabulary and expressions that you have learned empowers you to communicate effectively in various social, travel, and professional situations.

Furthermore, the incorporation of cultural nuances and idiomatic expressions has not only enriched your language proficiency but has also fostered a genuine appreciation for the diverse German-speaking world. Beyond just words and grammar, you've delved into the essence of communication, learning not only how to speak German but also how to connect with others on a deeper level.

As we bid farewell to this conversational journey, let's carry forward the confidence gained from these dialogues into your real-life interactions. May the conversations continue to flow, bridging linguistic and cultural gaps, and may the spirit of learning and curiosity propel us to further explore the captivating world of the German language and culture. Bis zum nächsten Gespräch!

German Short Stories For

Language Learners

Learn and Improve Your German Comprehension and Vocabulary Through 20 Short Stories Based Off Captivating German History

Worldwide Nomad

DAS WISSENSCHAFTLICHE RÄTSEL

Germanien war ein Ort mit einfachen, friedliebenden Menschen. Die Männer und Frauen bewirtschafteten das Land und lehrten ihre Söhne und Töchter, Fische zu fangen und Perlen zu finden. Sie hatten mehr als genug zu essen und verkauften den Rest an benachbarte Dörfer. Eines Tages, als Julius Cäsar mit seinen Senatoren auf der Jagd war, entdeckte er dieses Land von weitem. Er sah die üppige Vegetation, die schönen Flüsse und die wertvollen Steine. Er begehrte das Land und wollte es zu einem Teil seines Reiches machen. Doch er konnte das Land nicht betreten. Es war durch eine riesige Schlucht vom Festland getrennt, und niemandem war es je gelungen, sie zu überwinden. Julius Cäsar rief alle Weisen und Wissenschaftler seines Reiches zusammen und befahl ihnen, an einer Vorrichtung zur Überquerung der Schlucht zu arbeiten. Die Wissenschaftler arbeiteten Tag und Nacht an der Schlucht, aber sie waren der Lösung nicht näher gekommen. Die Menschen in Germanien gingen ihren Geschäften nach und kümmerten sich nicht um die Aktivitäten von Julius Cäsars Wissenschaftlern auf der anderen Seite des Canyons. Schließlich drohte Julius Cäsar damit, alle seine Wissenschaftler ins Gefängnis zu werfen, wenn sie nicht eine Lösung finden würden. Ein weiser Mann, Kephas, traf sich mit einem Händler aus Germanien, der gekommen war, um landwirtschaftliche Produkte zu verkaufen, und verriet ihm das Geheimnis des Abstiegs ins Tal. Der weise Mann erzählte es Julius Cäsar, der ihn reich belohnte.

THE SCIENTIFIC CONUNDRUM

Germania was a place of simple, peace loving people. The men and women farmed the lands and they taught their sons and daughters to catch fishes and to find pearls. They had more than enough to eat and sold the rest to neighboring villages. One day, while on a hunting trip with his senators, Julius Caesar discovered this land from afar. He saw the lush vegetation, the beautiful rivers and the valuable stones. He coveted the land and wanted to make it part of his empire. However, he could not get into the land. It was divided from the mainland by a huge canyon and no one had ever succeeded in crossing it. Julius Caesar called together all the wise men and scientist in his kingdom and commanded them to start working on an equipment to cross the canyon. The scientists worked day and night by the canyon but they were no closer to finding a solution. The people of Germania went about their businesses, not caring about the activities of Julius Caesar's scientist on the other side of the Canyon. Finally, Julius Caesar threatened to throw all his scientists in prison if they did not come up with a solution. A wise man, Cephas, met with a trader from Germania who had come to sell farm produce and tricked him into telling the secret of descending into the valley. The wise man told Julius Caesar who rewarded him greatly.

VOCABULARY

Einfach - Simple
Frauen - Women
Fluss - Foolish
Menschen - People
Stein - Stone
Händler - Trader
Reise - Trip
Frieden - Peace
Land - Land
Ort - Place
Üppige - Lush
Genug - Enough
Nacht - Night
Canyon - Canyon

COMPREHENSION QUESTIONS

Wie lebten die Menschen in Germanien? How did the people of Germania live?

Warum wollte Julius Cäsar nach Germanien gehen? Why did Julius Caesar want to go into Germania?

Wie entdeckte Julius Cäsar das Geheimnis der Einreise nach Germanien? How did Julius Caesar discover the secret of entering Germania?

HISTORICAL NOTE

Germania was a region in north-central Europe during the Roman era. The name, Germani, was first given to the people of a north-central region in Europe by Roman General Julius Caesar after he encountered them originating from beyond the Rhine. He called them Germani and their land, Germania.

VERTRAUEN MIßBRAUCHT

Arminius arbeitete als Diener im Haushalt des römischen Generals Quinctilius Varus. Er war so fleißig, dass Varus von ihm beeindruckt war und ihn als Teil seiner Hauswache ausbilden ließ, obwohl Arminius ein Angehöriger der Germanen war. Die germanischen Stämme waren eingeschworene Feinde der Römer, die sie ständig in Konflikte verwickelten. Aber Varus, der keinen eigenen Sohn hatte, war von dem brillanten und fleißigen Arminius so angetan. Schon bald beförderte er Arminius von der Hauswache zu einem Soldaten unter seinem Kommando. Er vertraute Arminius so sehr, dass er ihn in den Kriegstaktiken der römischen Armee unterrichtete. Er half ihm auch, das römische Bürgerrecht zu erwerben. Nach einiger Zeit kam es zu einem weiteren Angriff der Germanen auf die römischen Soldaten, der sich zu einem Krieg ausweitete. Die Römer trafen Vorbereitungen und waren sich des Sieges sicher. Sie planten, die Germanen auf einem bestimmten Hügel anzugreifen, wo sie lagerten, aber als die römische Armee dorthin marschierte, waren die Germanen bereits verschwunden. Die verwirrten Römer wurden von hinten angegriffen und verloren die Schlacht. Arminius schloss sich den Germanen an, um gegen die Römer zu kämpfen, und offenbarte dem untröstlichen Varus, dass er den Germanen die Strategie der Römer verraten hatte.

BETRAYAL

Arminius worked as a servant in the roman general, Quinctilius Varus' household. He was so diligent that Varus was impressed by him and let him receive training as part of his house guard even though Arminius was a member of the Germanic tribes. The Germanic tribes were sworn enemies of the Romans and they constantly engaged them in conflict. But Varus who didn't have a son of his own was so endeared by brilliant and hardworking Arminius. He soon promoted Arminius from house guard to a soldier under his command. He trusted Arminius so much that he taught him the war tactics of the Roman army. He also helped him acquire a roman citizenship. After some time, there was another attack on the Roman soldiers by the Germanic tribes and it grew into a war. The Romans made preparations and they were sure of victory. They planned to attack the Germanic tribes at a certain hill where they were camped but when the Roman army marched there, the Germanic tribes were gone. The confused Romans were attacked from behind and lost the battle. Arminius joined the Germanic tribes to fight the Romans and revealed to a heartbroken Varus that he told the Germanic tribes the strategy of the Romans.

VOCABULARY

Diener - Servant
Hügel - Hill
Stamm - Tribe
Krieg - War
Verloren - Lost
Kämpfen - Fight
Befehl - Command
Sohn - Son
Erwerben Sie - Acquire
Konflikt - Conflict
Sieg - Victory
Angreifen - Attack
Beeindruckt - Impressed
Glänzend - Brillant
Fleißig - Diligent

COMPREHENSION QUESTIONS

Was war Arminius' ursprünglicher Beruf? What was Arminius's initial occupation?

Wie verdiente Arminius das Wohlwollen des Varus? How did Arminius merit Varus' goodwill?

Warum war Varus untröstlich? Why was Varus heartbroken?

HISTORICAL NOTE

The Battle of the Teutoburg Forest was a major battle between the Germanic tribes and the Roman Empire. An alliance of Germanic tribes led by Arminius, a Germanic officer of Varus's auxilia, ambushed three Roman legions led by Quinctilius Varus.

DER CHAOS SÄENDE HÄNDLER

In der Stadt Mount Souri waren die Menschen der Herrschaft des Römischen Reiches überdrüssig und wollten sich selbst regieren. Der Berg Souri war eine der Provinzen des westlichen Teils des Römischen Reiches. Ein alter und wohlhabender Kaufmann, Philipus, versicherte dem Rat von Mount Souri, dass er wisse, wie man sie aus der römischen Herrschaft befreien könne. Er reiste mit einigen anderen reichen Kaufleuten vom Berg Souri in die Hauptstadt und besuchte den Königshof. Dort stellte er fest, dass viele der Senatoren mit dem Kaiser unzufrieden waren und ihn ablösen wollten. Viele von ihnen begehrten sogar den Thron. Philipus traf sich mit verschiedenen Senatoren und versprach ihnen, sie zu unterstützen. Er machte sie untereinander misstrauisch und stiftete sie zum Kampf an. In der Hauptstadt brach ein Bürgerkrieg aus, bei dem verschiedene Adelshäuser einzelne Senatoren im Kampf um den Thron unterstützten. Während die Menschen in der Hauptstadt durch den anhaltenden Konflikt abgelenkt waren, reiste Philipus zurück zum Berg Souri und organisierte die Geheimarmee der Stadt. Sie schlossen sich mit den anderen Provinzen des Weströmischen Reiches zusammen und bekämpften die römische Armee in ihren Städten. Sie besiegten sie erfolgreich und wurden vom Römischen Reich befreit.

THE CHAOS SOWING MERCHANT

In the city of Mount Souri, the people were tired of domination by the Roman Empire and wanted to govern themselves. Mount Souri was one of the provinces under the Western part of the Roman Empire. An old and wealthy merchant, Philipus, assured the Mount Souri council that he knew how to get them out from under Roman rule. He traveled to the capital with some other rich merchants of Mount Souri and visited the royal court. There he discovered that many of the senators were displeased with the Emperor and wanted to replace him. Many of them in face coveted the throne. Philipus met with different senators and promised to support them. He made them suspicious of each other and instigated them to fighting. A civil war broke out in the capital, with different noble houses supporting individual senators for the throne. While the people in the capital were distracted by the ongoing conflict, Philipus traveled back to Mount Souri and organized the city's secret army. They formed an alliance with the other provinces of the Western Roman Empire and fought the Roman army in their cities. They successfully defeated them and were free from the Roman Empire.

VOCABULARY

Stadt - City
Verdächtig - Suspicious
Bereist - Traveled
Frei - Free
Abgelenkt - Distracted
Unterstützung - Support
Thron - Throne
Besucht - Visited
Reich - Rich
Ersetzen - Replaced
Armee - Army
Unzufrieden - Displeased
Königlich - Royal
Vorherrschaft - Domination
Von - From

COMPREHENSION QUESTION

Welche Strategie wandte Philippus an, um die Freiheit des Berges Souri zu sichern?
What strategy did Philipus use to secure Mount Souri's freedom?

Was führte zu dem Bürgerkrieg in der Hauptstadt? What led to the civil war in the capital?

Was dachten die Senatoren über den Kaiser? How did the senators feel about the emperor?

HISTORICAL NOTE

The fall of the Western Roman Empire was a gradual loss of the Roman Empire's political control in its western provinces. This process was credited to many reasons including the strength of the Roman economy, the effectiveness of the army, the competence of the emperors, and internal power struggles.

TAPFERKEIT IN DER FALSCHEN WENDUNG

Während die Bewohner des Berges Souri und der anderen Provinzen im Westen ihre Freiheit feierten, schmiedeten die Franken Pläne für einen Angriff auf sie. Die Franken sahen in der Ablenkung und der gerade errungenen Freiheit eine Chance und rüsteten ihre Armeen für eine feindliche Übernahme der Provinzen. Eines Morgens wachten die Bewohner des Berges Souri auf und sahen ein großes Heer, das auf einem Hügel nicht weit von ihrer Stadt lagerte. Die Ältesten der Gemeinde eilten sofort zu ihrem neuen König, einem jungen Mann namens Achaios. Sie fragten König Achaios, was er in dieser Situation zu tun gedenke, und er erklärte, dass er gegen die Franken kämpfen werde. Die Ältesten versuchten, ihn zu warnen, da die Franken ein zehnmal größeres Heer hatten als sie selbst, aber er wollte nicht hören. Er berief eine Versammlung aller Bürger ein und teilte ihnen mit, dass sie gegen die Invasionsarmee kämpfen würden. Das Volk war von seinen mutigen Worten begeistert und entschlossen, zu kämpfen. Die erste Schlacht gegen die Franken machte jedoch deutlich, dass sie den Krieg nicht gewinnen konnten. Viele Menschen verloren ihr Leben, und das Volk gab dem König die Schuld. Die Ältesten kamen zusammen und fassten den Beschluss, die Stadt zu retten. Sie trafen sich mit den fränkischen Herrschern und handelten vorteilhafte Bedingungen für eine Kapitulation aus.

BRAVERY AT THE WRONG TURN

As the people of Mount Souri and the other provinces in the West were celebrating their freedom, the Franks made plans to attack them. The Franks saw an opportunity in their distraction and their recent freedom and they readied their armies for a hostile takeover of these provinces. One morning, the people of Mount Souri woke up and saw a great army camped at a hill not so distant from their city. The elders of the community immediately rushed to meet their new king, a young man named Achaius. They asked King Achaius what he intended to do about the situation and he declared that he would fight the Franks. The elders tried to caution him, as the Franks had an army that was ten times larger than theirs but he would not listen. He called an assembly of all citizens and informed them that they would fight the invading army. The people were excited by his courageous words and determined to fight. The first battle against the Franks, however, made it clear that they could not win the war. A lot of lives were lost and the people blamed the King. The elders came together and made a decision to save the city. They met with the Frankish rulers and negotiated favorable terms of surrender.

VOCABULARY

Freiheit - Freedom
Pläne - Plans
Feiern Sie - Celebrate
Feindlich - Hostile
Gelegenheit - Opportunity
Vorsicht - Caution
Mutig - Courageous
Zuhören - Listen
Entschlossen - Determined
Größer - Larger
Eindringen - Invading
Klar - Clear
Verhandeln - Negotiate
Entscheidung - Decision

COMPREHENSION QUESTIONS

Wie hat König Achaios die Situation gemeistert? How did King Achaius handle the situation?

Wie hat das Volk auf die Niederlage reagiert? What was the people's reaction to defeat?

Was taten die Ältesten, um die Situation zu retten? What did the elders do to salvage the situation?

HISTORICAL NOTE

The Kingdom of Franks was one of the last surviving Germanic kingdoms. It was also the largest post-Roman barbarian kingdom. After the fall of the Western Roman Empire, the Franks conquered other West Germanic Tribes.

DER HEILIGE RÖMISCHE KAISER

Schon in jungen Jahren wusste Karl der Große, dass er eines Tages König der Franken werden würde. Als er älter wurde, beobachtete er die Dinge um sich herum genau. Er bemerkte die wirtschaftliche Depression und die schlechte Lebensqualität, die in ganz Westeuropa herrschte. Er erkannte, dass dies eine Folge der politischen Instabilität war, und schwor sich, die Dinge zu ändern, wenn er den Thron besteigen würde. Als Karl der Große König der Franken wurde, begann er mit seiner Mission, die zerrissenen Länder zu vereinen. Zunächst stieß er bei den Bewohnern dieser Gebiete auf Ablehnung, doch langsam begann er, sie zu überzeugen. Er traf sich mit ihren Herrschern und schloss diplomatische Bündnisse, die sie zu einem Teil seiner fränkischen Reiche machten. An den Orten, an denen autoritäre Männer herrschten, besiegte er sie und befreite das Volk von ihnen. Er machte sie alle zu einem Teil seines Reiches. Doch einige Menschen in anderen Teilen Europas flüsterten Gerüchte über ihn. Sie nannten ihn einen Herrscher, der unrechtmäßig die Macht ergriffen hatte. Um diese Gerüchte zu bekämpfen, wandte er sich an den Papst, der ihn als einen Mann des Friedens anerkannte. Der Kaiser salbte ihn zum heiligen römischen Kaiser, und niemand wagte es, schlecht über ihn zu reden.

THE HOLY ROMAN EMPEROR

From a young age, Charlemagne knew he would become King of the Franks one day. As he grew older, he observed things around him closely. He noticed the economic depression and the bad quality of life that was prominent all around Western Europe. He saw that this was a result of political instability and vowed to change things when he ascended the throne. When Charlemagne became Kings of the Franks, he started his mission to unite the fractured lands. At first, the people of these places frowned at his concerns but slowly, he started to convince them. He met with their rulers and formed diplomatic alliances that made them a part of his Frankish kingdoms. In the places where authoritarian men rule, he defeated them and liberated the people from under them. He made them all a part of his kingdom. Yet, some people in other parts of Europe whispered rumors about him. They called him a ruler who seized power illegitimately. To combat these rumors he went to the Pope who recognized him as a man of peace. The Emperor anointed him as the holy Roman Emperor and nobody dared speak badly about him.

VOCABULARY

Leben - Life
Unter - Under
Gerücht - Rumor
Junge - Young
Macht - Power
Geflüster - Whispered
Teil - Part
Unerlaubt - Illegitimate
Um - Around
Langsam - Slowly
Wirtschaftlich - Economic
Dinge - Thing
Qualität - Quality
Ältere - Older
Alter - Age

COMPREHENSION QUESTIONS

Was war die Aufgabe Karls des Großen? What was Charlemagne's mission?

Welche Bedeutung hatte die Salbung Karls des Großen durch den Papst? What was the significance of the Pope anointing Charlemagne?

Wie machte Karl der Große das Volk zu einem Teil seines Reiches? How did Charlemagne make the people a part of his Kingdom?

HISTORICAL NOTE

The Holy Roman Empire of the German Nation, existing from 800 to 1806, was a complex political entity in Central Europe. It included parts of modern day Germany. Though dissolved, its historical influence shaped German culture and politics as Germany's identity and federal structure still bear traces of its legacy.

DIE PIRATEN VON LAZYTOWN

In der Ost- und Nordsee herrschte eine Gilde reicher Seeleute über den Seehandel. Sie waren ursprünglich Holzschnitzer aus einer kleinen deutschen Stadt, aber sie lernten, besonderes Holz zu schnitzen und bauten daraus Schiffe. Sie besaßen die größten und stärksten Schiffe und reisten in ferne Länder, um Seide, Gewürze und Gold zu beschaffen und zu verkaufen. Händler und Kaufleute wurden vom Hafen ihrer kleinen norddeutschen Stadt angezogen, die zu einem Drehkreuz für den Handel wurde. Der Lebensstandard der Stadtbewohner erhöhte sich erheblich, da sie mehr Geschäfte machten. Eines Tages wurden sie auf ihrer monatlichen Reise von einem Piratenschiff überfallen. All ihre Waren wurden gestohlen und ihre Schiffe waren schwer beschädigt. Aber die Schiffe waren aus starkem Holz gebaut und brachten sie sicher nach Hause zurück. Die Stadt erlitt einen großen Verlust durch diesen einen Angriff. Leider geschah dasselbe auf ihrer nächsten Reise. Man fand dies verdächtig und führte eine Untersuchung durch. Dabei fanden sie heraus, dass es sich bei den Piraten um Mitglieder einer rivalisierenden Stadt handelte, die zu faul waren, selbst Schiffe zu bauen oder auf Reisen zu gehen. Die Seemannsgilde heuerte starke Söldner an, um sie auf ihrer nächsten Reise zu beschützen. Sie besiegten die Piraten und wurden nicht mehr belästigt.

THE PIRATES OF LAZYTOWN

In the Baltic and North Seas, a guild of wealthy sailors held sway over the maritime trade. They were formerly wood carvers of a little German town but they learned to carve special wood and built ships out of them. They had the largest and strongest ships and traveled to far places to procure silk, spices, and gold for sale. Traders and merchants were attracted to the port of their little North German town and it became a hub for trade. The standard of living of the town dwellers was greatly increased as they got more business. One day while on their monthly voyage, they were attacked by a pirate ship. All their goods were stolen and they their ships were badly broke. But the ships were made of strong wood and got them back home safe. The town suffered a great loss from this single attack. Sadly, the same thing happened on their next voyage. They found this suspicious and carried out an investigation. From their investigation they discovered that the pirates were no one else but members of a rival town who were too lazy to build ships or go on voyages themselves. The guild of sailors employed strong mercenaries to protect them on their next voyage. They defeated the pirates and they were no longer troubled.

VOCABULARY

Rivalen - Rival
Faule - Lazy
Gilde - Guild
Pirat - Pirate
Zuhause - Home
Schiff - Ship
Verkaufen - Sale
Beschaffen - Procure
Stark - Strong
Seemann - Sailor
Stadt - Town
Reise - Voyage
Nächste - Next
Besiegt - Defeat
Weiter - Far

COMPREHENSION QUESTIONS

Was machte die Wirtschaft der norddeutschen Stadt aus? What constituted the economy of the North German town?

Wie wurde die Identität der Seeräuber aufgedeckt? How was the identity of the pirates revealed?

Welche Lösung haben sie für das Piratenproblem gefunden? What solution did they employ to the pirate problem?

HISTORICAL NOTE

The Hanseatic League was an early medieval age commercial and defensive confederation of merchant guilds and market towns in Central and Northern Europe. It grew from a few North German towns but expanded to encompass 200 settlements and seven modern-day countries between the 13th and 15th centuries.

DIE KRIEGER DES FRIEDENS

Die Ritter des Deutschen Ordens waren eine Gruppe von jungen Männern, die von der deutschen katholischen Kirche gesalbt wurden. Sie waren eine militärische Truppe, die im Umgang mit Waffen geübt war. Ihre Aufgabe war es, religiösen Wallfahrten zu helfen, sie gegen Angriffe zu verteidigen und sich um andere Christen zu kümmern. Sie standen für Frieden, Schutz und Sicherheit. Es gab jedoch eine Gruppe unter ihnen, die mit ihrer Rolle in der Kirche nicht zufrieden war. Sie glaubten, sie sollten mehr Macht haben und die Kirche kontrollieren. Sie bekämpften die Leiter der Kirche und übernahmen von ihnen die Herrschaft über die Kirche. Dann gingen sie über die Kirche hinaus und begannen, die Menschen in den Städten mit Gewalt zum Christentum zu bekehren. Sie wurden immer zahlreicher und zogen umher, um andere Menschen für ihre Sache zu bekehren. Sie übernahmen gewaltsam Städte und bedrohten Länder, die sie nicht akzeptieren wollten, mit Krieg. Sie führten mehrere bewaffnete Auseinandersetzungen und konnten viele Länder erobern. Anschließend schlossen sie alle besiegten Länder zu einem Staat zusammen und nannten ihn Deutschordensstaat. Dies hielt jedoch nicht lange an, da sie sich nicht einmal untereinander einigen konnten, wer das Oberhaupt sein sollte. Am Ende bekämpften sie sich gegenseitig und der Deutschordensstaat wurde aufgelöst.

THE WARRIORS OF PEACE

The Knights of the Teutonic order were a group of young men who were anointed by the German Catholic Church. They were a military squad skilled in the use of weapons. Their duty was to help religious pilgrimages, defend them against attacks and take care of other Christians. They represented peace, protection and safety. However, there was a group among them who were not satisfied with their role in the church. They believed they should have more power and be in control of the church. They fought the leaders of the church and took over the rule of the church from them. Then they went beyond the church and started to make people in the towns forcibly convert to Christianity. They grew greatly in number as they went around, converting other people to their cause. They forcibly took over towns and threatened countries who would not accept them with war. They engaged in several armed conflicts and succeeded in conquering many countries. Then, they brought all the defeated countries together as one state and called it the State of the Teutonic Order. However, this did not last long as they could not even agree amongst themselves who would be the overall head. In the end, they fought each other and the State of the Teutonic Order was dissolved.

VOCABULARY

Ritter - Knight
Viele - Many
Militär - Military
Lang - Long
Rolle - Role
Verteidigen - Defend
Staat - State
Bekehren - Convert
Einverstanden - Agreed
Zufrieden - Satisfied
Ursache - Cause
Kader - Squad
Kirche - Church
Leitung - Head

COMPREHENSION QUESTIONS

Was war der ursprüngliche Zweck der Ritter des Deutschen Ordens? What was the original purpose of the Knights of the Teutonic Order?

Haben sie dieses Ziel erreicht? Did they achieve that purpose?

Was führte zur Auflösung des Deutschen Ordensstaates? What led to the dissolution of the State of the Teutonic Order?

HISTORICAL NOTE

The State of the Teutonic Order was a theocratic state formed by the Knights of the Teutonic Order. The Order of Brothers of the German House of Saint Mary was a catholic religious institution that was created as a military society. It was founded to aid Christians on their pilgrimage to Jerusalem and to establish hospitals and its members were referred to as the Teutonic Knights. This moniker came from their time as military crusaders for the catholic rule in Jerusalem.

DAS MACHTGERANGEL

Es war die Zeit des Jahres, in der neue Bischöfe ernannt wurden. Normalerweise war diese Zeit mit vielen religiösen Feiern verbunden und brachte Freude in die Herzen vieler Menschen, aber dieses Mal war es anders. Das Land war gespannt auf den Konflikt, über den niemand offen sprechen wollte. Es gab Gerüchte, dass sich der Papst und der König im Krieg befänden und deshalb am festgelegten Datum keine Bischöfe ernannt würden. Das hatte es noch nie gegeben, und die Menschen machten sich Sorgen, was dies bedeuten würde. Ein weiser alter Mann, Jude, lud den Papst in sein Haus ein und lud auch den König heimlich ein, ohne dass einer der beiden davon wusste. Als Jude und der Papst sich zum Essen hinsetzten, kam der König herein. Beide begannen eine Schimpftirade, aber Jude warnte sie. Er scheute sich nicht, sie auf ihr kindisches Verhalten hinzuweisen, obwohl sie die beiden mächtigsten Männer der Stadt waren. Er fragte sie nach dem Grund ihres Streits, und der Papst teilte ihm mit, dass der König die Bischöfe ernennen wolle. Er wies darauf hin, dass dies unmöglich sei, da er als Papst am besten wisse, wer als Bischof in Frage komme. Der König äußerte seine Besorgnis darüber, dass die Bischöfe dem Papst und nicht dem Land gegenüber loyal sein könnten. Judas lachte über dieses Argument und schlug eine einfache Lösung vor: Der Papst würde die Bischöfe ernennen und die Bischöfe würden dem König die Treue schwören. Der Papst und der König stimmten zu, und nachdem der Streit beigelegt war, setzten sie sich zu einem Essen mit Jude zusammen, um wieder Freunde zu werden.

THE POWER TUSSLE

It was that time in the year when new bishops were appointed. Usually, this time came with a lot of religious celebrations and brought joy to the hearts of many but this time it was different. The country was tense with excitement for the conflict that no one would openly speak about. There were rumors going about that the Pope and the King were at war and so no bishops would be appointed on the set date. This had never before happened and people worried about what this would mean. A wise old man, Jude, invited the Pope to his house and also secretly invited the King without either of them knowing. As Jude and the Pope sat down to eat, the King came in. They both burst into a tirade of insults but Jude cautioned them. He was not afraid to point out their childish behavior although they were the two most powerful men in town. He asked them for the point of their conflict and the Pope informed him that the King wanted to appoint the bishops. He pointed out that this was impossible because he as the Pope knew best who was eligible to be bishop. The King voiced his worries about the bishops been loyal to the Pope instead of the country. Jude laughed at their argument and proposed a simple solution: the Pope would appoint the bishops and the bishops would swear fealty to the King. The Pope and the King agreed and with the dispute settled, they ate sat down to a meal with Jude as friends once again.

VOCABULARY

Loyal -Loyal
Essen - Eat
Feiern - Celebration
Freude - Joy
Freunde - Friends
Angst - Afraid
Herz - Heart
Wählbar - Eligible
Neu - New
Mächtig - Powerful
Zeit - Time
Lösung - Solution
Anspannung - Tense
Argument - Argument

COMPREHENSION QUESTIONS

Warum war das Volk beunruhigt? Why were the people worried?

Was war der Grund für die Meinungsverschiedenheit zwischen dem König und dem Papst? What was the basis of the King's disagreement with the Pope?

Wie wurde die Meinungsverschiedenheit beigelegt? How was the disagreement resolved?

HISTORICAL NOTE

The Investiture Controversy was an 11th and 12th century conflict between the papacy and secular rulers. It revolved around the appointment of bishops and abbots. The church claimed the sole right to appoint them, while emperors and kings sought influence over these appointments.

LIEBE IN RAUEN ZEITEN

Maria wuchs damit auf, dass ihre Mutter in ihrem kleinen Dorf als Heilerin arbeitete. Als sie älter wurde, begann sie, im Heilungszelt zu assistieren, und als ihre Mutter starb, übernahm sie diese Aufgabe. Im Alter von achtzehn Jahren war sie eine geschickte Heilerin, die das, was sie von ihrer Mutter gelernt hatte, mit einer persönlichen Ausbildung kombinierte, die sie in Angriff nahm. Sie war so geschickt im Heilen, dass die Menschen aus den umliegenden Städten zu ihr kamen. Obwohl sie nie Geld für ihre Dienste verlangte, sorgten die Menschen dafür, dass es ihr nie an etwas fehlte. Sie machten ihr Geschenke, schickten ihr Kinder, die ihr bei der Hausarbeit halfen, und brachten ihr Essen. Auch viele junge Männer fühlten sich zu ihr hingezogen. Sie kamen von nah und fern, um um ihre Hand anzuhalten, aber sie lehnte ab. Eines Tages brach plötzlich ein Krieg aus, und Maria fand sich mittendrin wieder und heilte verwundete Soldaten und unschuldige Zivilisten, die in die Kämpfe verwickelt waren. In dieser Zeit lernte sie Erik, einen jungen Soldaten, kennen. Obwohl sie die Soldaten nicht mochte, weil sie den Krieg herbeigeführt hatten, konnte sie nicht umhin, sich in Erik und seine sanfte Art zu verlieben. Sie überzeugte ihn davon, nicht mehr zu kämpfen, und er half ihr stattdessen, die unschuldigen Menschen zu heilen, die unter den Folgen des Krieges litten.

LOVE IN HARSH TIMES

Maria grew up watching her mother work as a healer in their little village. As she grew older she started to assist in the healing tent and when her mother passed on, she took on the job. At the age of eighteen she was a skilled healer who combined the things she learned from her mother with personal education she embarked on. She was so skilled at healing that people came to her from surrounding towns. Although she never charged for her services, people made sure she never lacked. They would give her gifts, send children to help her with house chores and bring her food. Many young men found themselves drawn to her as well. They came from far and wide to seek her hand in marriage but she refused. One day, war broke out all of a sudden and Maria found herself in the middle of it, healing wounded soldiers and innocent civilians who were caught in the fighting. It was at this time that she met Erik, a young soldier. Although she disliked the soldiers for bringing war, she couldn't help but fall in love with Erik and his gentle manner. She convinced him to quit fighting and he instead helped her with healing the innocent people who suffered the brunt of the war.

VOCABULARY

Mutter - Mother
Heilerin - Healer
Zelt - Tent
Beruf - Job
Geschickt - Skilled
Kündigen - Quit
Liebe - Love
Persönlich - Personal
Senden - Send
Geschenke - Gifts
Soldat - Soldier
Kinder - Children
Gefangene - Caught
Dienstleistungen - Services

COMPREHENSION QUESTIONS

Wie hat Maria Erik kennengelernt? How did Maria meet Erik?

Wie sahen die Menschen Maria? How did the people view Maria?

Wie war Marias Reaktion auf den Krieg? What was Maria's reaction to the war?

HISTORICAL NOTE

The origin of the Thirty Years' War is linked to the deposition of Emperor Ferdinand II as King of Bohemia and his replacement by the Protestant Fredrick V of the Palatinate. This led to a revolt and to fighting in the Palatinate. Other states like the Dutch Republic and Spain got involved, leading to an escalation of the conflict.

DER TAG DER MUTTER CELIA

Während des langen Dreißigjährigen Krieges im Heiligen Römischen Reich waren die Menschen sehr müde, und auch die Soldaten hatten keine Kraft mehr zum Kämpfen. Alle riefen nach Frieden, aber leider konnte niemand die beiden Seiten dazu bringen, sich zu treffen und zu einigen. Eines Tages erschien eine seltsame und uralte Frau namens Celia in der Stadt. Niemand hatte sie zuvor gesehen, aber sie schien nicht neu an diesem Ort zu sein. Sie ging geradewegs zu den Kasernen der einzelnen Kriegsführer. Sie zerrte sie an den Ohren und brachte sie in eine Baumhöhle. Sie zwang sie, sich zusammenzusetzen und den Krieg zu besprechen. Sie befahl ihnen, sich zu einigen, bevor die Sonne unterging. Die beiden Kriegsführer sprachen eine Weile, und noch vor Sonnenuntergang entließen beide ihre Armeen und erklärten den Krieg für beendet. Beide unterzeichneten Dokumente, die besagten, dass sie nie wieder gegeneinander Krieg führen würden. Die Menschen begannen zu jubeln und suchten nach Celia, um ihr zu danken, aber sie war spurlos verschwunden. Sie kamen zu dem Schluss, dass Celia ein Engel sein musste, und stellten überall in der Stadt Statuen von ihr auf. Von diesem Tag an feierten sie diesen Tag jedes Jahr als den Tag der Mutter Celia.

THE DAY OF MOTHER CELIA

During the long Thirty Years' War in the Holy Roman Empire, the people were greatly tired and even the soldiers had no more strength for fighting. Everyone clamored for peace but sadly, no one could get the two sides to meet and agree. One day, a strange and ancient woman named Celia appeared in town. No one had seen her previously but she did not seem new to the place. She headed straight to the army barracks of each of the war leaders. She dragged them by ears and brought them into a groove of trees. She made them to sit together and discuss the war. She ordered them to come to an agreement before the sun went down. The two war leaders spoke for a while and before sunset they both dismissed their armies and declared the end of the war. They both signed documents that said that they would not go to war against each other again. People began to jubilate and searched for Celia to thank her but she was gone without a trace. They concluded that Celia must be an angel and they erected statues of her all around town. From that day forward, they celebrated that day every year as the Day of Mother Celia.

VOCABULARY

Müde - Tired
Dokumente - Documents
Unterschreiben - Sign
Beide - Both
Verfolgen - Trace
Jubilate - Jubilate
Danken - Thank
Ohne - Without
Zusammen - Together
Diskutieren - Discuss
Jeder - Each
Stärke - Strength
Vereinbaren - Agree
Antike - Ancient

COMPREHENSION QUESTIONS

Wie lange dauerte der Krieg? How long did the war last?

Woher kam Celia? Where did Celia come from?

Wie hat das Volk seine Dankbarkeit gegenüber Celia ausgedrückt? How did the people express their gratitude to Celia?

HISTORICAL NOTE

The Peace of Westphalia is the name given to the two treaties signed in October 1648 in the two Westphalia cities. These treaties signified the official end of the Thirty Years' War.

FRANZISKUS DER VORNEHME

In den 1800er Jahren wurde das Heilige Römische Reich vom sanften Franz II. regiert. Er hatte einen freundlichen und großzügigen Geist, aber er war kein guter Politiker. Seine Untergebenen nutzten dies aus und manipulierten ihn, um Entscheidungen zu ihren Gunsten zu treffen. Franz II. erkannte, dass er als Anführer versagte, und beschloss, das zu tun, was sein Volk glücklich machen würde. Eines Tages ging er als einfacher Bürger verkleidet in die Stadt und fragte die Menschen, die er traf, was sie von der Regierung hielten. Sie alle beschwerten sich über das feudale Regierungssystem, das sie an einen reichen Grundbesitzer band. Sie wollten nicht ihr ganzes Leben lang für die Grundbesitzer arbeiten. Als Franz II. in seinen Palast zurückkehrte, ließ er verkünden, dass nun alle Menschen unter seiner Regierung Anspruch auf Land hätten und niemand mehr anderen Grundbesitzern dienen müsse. Viele Menschen freuten sich darüber, andere nicht. Ihnen gefiel das alte System. Andere wiederum wollten ein völlig anderes System. Franziskus erkannte, dass niemals alle dasselbe wollen würden, und er erließ ein weiteres Dekret. Er löste das Heilige Königliche Reich auf und errichtete daraus Unterstaaten. Er erlaubte den Menschen, sich dem Staat anzuschließen, der das System praktizierte, das ihnen gefiel. Dann gab er seine Krone auf und trat als Heiliger Römischer Kaiser zurück.

FRANCIS THE GENTEEL

In the 1800s the Holy Roman Empire was ruled by the gentle Francis II. He had a kind and generous spirit but he was not much of a politician. His subordinates would take advantage of this and manipulate him into taking decisions that favored them. Francis II realized he was failing as a leader and decided to do what would make his people happy. He went into town one day, disguised as an ordinary citizen and asked the people he met what they thought of the government. They all complained about the feudal system of government, which made them bound to a wealthy land owner. They did not want to spend all their lives working for the land owners. When Francis II returned to his palace, he sent out an announcement that all people would now be entitled to land under his government and nobody would have to serve other land owners. Many people were happy about it but others were not. They liked the old system. Other people wanted an entirely different system. Francis realized everyone would never like the same thing so he made another decree. He dissolved the Holy Royal Empire and set up under states from it. He allowed the people to join whichever state practiced the system they enjoyed. Then, he gave up his crown and stepped down as the Holy Roman Emperor.

VOCABULARY

Sanft - Gentle
Erlauben - Allow
Erlass - Decree
Entitled - Entitled
Andere - Another
Vorteil - Advantage
Viel - Much
Manipulieren - Manipulate
Glücklich - Happy
Verkleidet - Disguised
Geist - Spirit
Großzügig - Generous
Niemals - Never
Praktiziert - Practiced

COMPREHENSION QUESTIONS

Wie hat Franz II. sein Reich regiert? How did Francis II rule his empire?

Welche Lektion hat Franz II. nach seinem Abenteuer gelernt? What lesson did Francis II learn after his adventure?

Wie würden Sie Franz beschreiben? How would you describe Francis?

HISTORICAL NOTE

The dissolution of the Holy Roman Empire happened on 6th August 1806 when Francis II, the last Holy Roman Emperor, abdicated his title and released all imperial states and officials from their oaths and obligations to the empire, bringing an end to the thousand year empire.

DER DEUTSCHE BUNDESSTAAT

Nach dem Zerfall des Heiligen Römischen Reiches waren viele Menschen verwirrt. Sie wussten nicht, wohin sie gehörten, da sich Menschen mit der gleichen Ideologie zu unabhängigen Nationen zusammenschlossen, die andere ausschlossen. Zu dieser Zeit gab es eine Frau, Adele, die eine andere Ideologie vertrat als ihr Mann und ihre engen Freunde. Sie wollte weder von ihnen getrennt werden noch ihren Glauben ändern. Adele rief eine Gruppe von Menschen zusammen und schlug eine neue Methode zur Bildung ihrer Nationen vor. Sie schlug vor, dass Menschen, die dieselbe oder eine sehr ähnliche Sprache sprachen, derselben Nation angehören sollten. Sie würden alle verschiedene Staaten sein, die auf ihren individuellen Überzeugungen basierten, aber jeder Staat würde sich zu einer Nation zusammenschließen. Allen gefiel Adeles Idee und sie stimmten ihr sofort zu. Auf diese Weise konnte jeder mit seinen Lieben zusammenleben und trotzdem seine persönlichen Überzeugungen beibehalten.

THE GERMAN CONFEDERATION

After the dissolution of the Holy Roman Empire, many people were left confused. They had no idea where they belonged to as people with the same ideology came together to form independent nations that excluded others. At this time, there was a woman Adele who had a different ideology from her husband and her close friends. She didn't want to be parted from them neither did she want to change her belief. Adele called a group of people together and suggested a new method of forming their nations. She suggested that people that spoke the same or very similar languages should belong to the same nation. They would all be different states based on their individual beliefs but each state would come together to form a nation. Everyone liked Adele's idea and they immediately agreed to it. This way everyone could live with their loved ones and still uphold their personal beliefs.

VOCABULARY

Link - Left
Zugehörigkeit - Belong
Idee - Idea
Ideologie - Ideology
Schließen - Close
Anders - Different
Glaube - Belief
Auflösung - Dissolution
Nation - Nation
Aufrechterhaltung - Uphold
Weder - Neither
Methode - Method
Formular - Form
Ausgeschlossen - Excluded

COMPREHENSION QUESTIONS

Was war Adeles Dilemma? What was Adele's dilemma?

Welche Lösung schlug sie vor? What solution did she propose?

Wie haben die Menschen diese Lösung aufgenommen? How did people receive this solution?

HISTORICAL NOTE

The German Confederation was a group of 39 sovereign states in central Europe where German was the predominantly spoken language. It was created by the Congress of Vienna in 1815 as a substitute for the Holy Roman Empire.

HELLES GEISTER

Mahler war ein junger Mann, der in Deutschland lebte. Er verbrachte die meisten seiner Tage damit, die Welt zu studieren und über Büchern zu brüten. Während er die Welt um sich herum beobachtete, begann er über Möglichkeiten nachzudenken, wie man Dinge effizienter und mit weniger Zeitaufwand erledigen könnte. Er begann, diese Möglichkeiten zu erforschen und traf sich mit anderen Menschen, die ähnliche Interessen hatten. Schließlich hatte er eine Idee: eine Maschine, die Getreide in kürzester Zeit verarbeiten und verpacken kann und dafür sorgt, dass die Produkte lange lagerfähig sind. Er stellte seinen Entwurf vielen Getreideunternehmen vor, aber sie hielten ihn nicht für realistisch. Eines Tages traf er Abraham, den Besitzer eines heruntergekommenen Getreideunternehmens. Abraham stimmte zu, die Entwicklung dieser Maschine zu finanzieren, und als sie fertig war, wurde sein Getreide schneller verarbeitet und von den Verbrauchern bevorzugt. Andere Hersteller wurden darauf neidisch und baten Mahler, Maschinen für sie zu entwickeln, aber Mahler hatte sich anderen Dingen zugewandt. Er entwickelte Maschinen für die Verarbeitung von Früchten, für die Herstellung von Textilien und für andere Arten von Fertigprodukten. Bald nahm die Regierung Kontakt zu ihm auf und bat ihn um Zusammenarbeit, um die Produktion und die Wirtschaftskraft des Landes zu steigern.

BRIGHT MINDS

Mahler was a young man who lived in Germany. He spent most of his days studying the world and poring over books. As he observed the world around him, he began to think of ways in which things could be done more efficiently and spending lesser time. He started looking into this possibility and met with other people who had similar interests. Finally, he came up with an idea: a machine that could process and package grain in little time and ensure that the products can be stored for a long time. He took his design to many grain companies but they did not think it was realistic. One day, he met Abraham, the owner of a rundown grain company. Abraham agreed to give funding to create this machine and when it was created his grains became faster processed and more preferred among the consumers. Other manufacturers grew jealous of this and they begged Mahler to design machines for them but Mahler had moved on to other things. He went on to create machines that could process fruits, make textiles and other kinds of finished products. Soon, the government contacted him and asked him to work with them in order to increase the country's production and economic power.

VOCABULARY

Die meisten - Most
Bücher - Books
Welt - World
Rund um - Around
Beobachtet - Observed
Getreide - Grain
Eifersüchtig - Jealous
Produkt - Product
Textil - Textile
Fertiges - Finished
Obst - Grain
Bevorzugt - Jealous
Maschine - Product
Eigentümer - Preferred
Unternehmen - Machine

COMPREHENSION QUESTIONS

Was war die Vision von Mahler? What was Mahler's vision?

Warum wollten die anderen Unternehmen plötzlich seine Entwürfe? Why did the other companies suddenly want his designs?

Wie hat er zur Wirtschaft seines Landes beigetragen? How did he contribute to his country's economy?

HISTORICAL NOTE

The industrial revolution was a period of worldwide innovation. It saw the change in human economy towards efficient and stable manufacturing processes. It went from hand production methods to the use of machines, new chemical manufacturing and iron production processes.

BRUDERSCHAFT

Die süddeutschen Staaten und die norddeutschen Staaten standen in ständiger Konkurrenz zueinander. Sie versuchten immer zu beweisen, wer die bessere Kultur und die bessere Sprachbeherrschung hatte. Dann, eines Tages, begann ein großer Vulkan in Süddeutschland Rauch aufzusteigen. Die Menschen in Süddeutschland waren sehr verängstigt und wussten nicht, wohin sie gehen sollten. Die Führer Norddeutschlands hielten eine Versammlung ab und äußerten ihre Besorgnis über den Vulkan. Sassaro, einer der Anführer, schlug vor, den Vulkan zu ignorieren und die Süddeutschen sterben zu lassen, da sie seit langem mit ihnen rivalisierten. Andere Anführer sprachen sich jedoch gegen diesen Vorschlag aus. Sie wiesen darauf hin, dass die Süddeutschen mit ihnen verwandt seien, da sie eine ähnliche Kultur hätten und dieselbe Sprache sprächen. Sie schickten eine Einladung an die Führer Süddeutschlands und baten sie, in ihren Städten zu leben, bis die Bedrohung durch den Vulkan beseitigt war. Die Süddeutschen waren besorgt darüber, inmitten ihrer langjährigen Rivalen zu leben, aber sie hatten keine andere Wahl. Sie waren überrascht von der Gastfreundschaft, die sie in Norddeutschland erfuhren. Sie blieben lange Zeit dort, arbeiteten und lebten ihr gewohntes Leben. Als die Bedrohung durch den Vulkan ohne Zwischenfälle vorüberging, war es für die Südländer an der Zeit, nach Hause zurückzukehren, aber sie wollten nicht gehen. Auch die Nordländer wollten sich nicht von ihren neuen Freunden trennen. Schließlich beschlossen sie, ein Land zu werden und frei zusammenzuleben.

BROTHERHOOD

The southern German states and the northern German states were in constant competition with each other. They always sought to prove who had the better culture and a better linguistic grasp of the language. Then, one day, a large volcano in southern Germany started to send up smoke. The people of southern Germany were very scared and had no idea where to go. The leaders of Northern Germany held a meeting and expressed their concerns about the volcano. Sassaro, one of the leaders, suggested that they ignore it and let the southern Germans die as they were their long time rival. However, other leaders spoke against this. They pointed out that the southern Germans were their kin as they had similar cultures and spoke the same language. They sent an invite to the leaders of south Germany and asked them to live in their cities until the threat of the volcano was solved. The people of South Germany worried about living amidst their long time rivals but they had no choice. They were surprised at the hospitality they received in North Germany. They stayed there for a long time, working and living their usual lives. When the threat of the volcano passed without incident, the time came for the southerners to return home but they did not want to go. The northerners did not want to part with their new friends either. Finally, they decided to become one country and live together freely.

VOCABULARY

Konstante - Constant
Jede - Each
Immer - Always
Besser - Better
Wettbewerb - Competition
Verängstigt - Scared
Treffen - Meeting
Gegen - Against
Verwandtschaft - Kin
Rivalen - Rival
Auswahl - Choice
Überrascht - Surprised
Zurückkehren - Return
Einladen - Invite
Bedrohung - Threat

COMPREHENSION QUESTIONS

Welcher Gefahr waren die Süddeutschen ausgesetzt? What danger did the Southern German face?

Wie haben die Norddeutschen ihnen geholfen? How did the Northerners assist them?

Was ergab sich aus ihrer unwahrscheinlichen Freundschaft? What resulted from their unlikely friendship?

HISTORICAL NOTE

The Unification of Germany refers to the process of creating the first nation-state for Germans. This state had federal features based on the concept of Lesser Germany. It started on 18th August with the adoption of the North German Confederation Treaty.

DEUTSCHLAND IN DER NEUEN WELT

Als Otto von Bismarck, der deutsche Reichskanzler, feststellte, wie viel Gewinn die Briten und Franzosen mit der Ausbeutung afrikanischer Gebiete machten, beschloss er, sich an dem Wettlauf um überseeische Gebiete zu beteiligen. Er befürchtete, dass die Briten und Franzosen mächtiger werden könnten als Deutschland, und wollte daher mehr Reichtum erwerben. Er schickte seine Armeen in verschiedene Gebiete und unterwarf die Menschen erfolgreich, bis sie nach Burundi kamen. In den anderen Gebieten, die sie eroberten, führten sie bewaffnete Auseinandersetzungen mit den Menschen oder verhandelten mit ihren Führern, aber in Burundi trafen sie auf niemanden. Wann immer die Menschen ihre Annäherung bemerkten, rannten sie tief in den Wald, wo die deutsche Armee nicht hingehen konnte, ohne sich zu verirren. Sie suchten weiter nach den Menschen, fanden sie aber nicht. Schließlich gaben sie auf und kehrten nach Deutschland zurück.

GERMANY IN THE NEW WORLD

When Otto von Bismarck, the German Chancellor noted how much profit the British and the French were making by exploiting African territories, he decided to join in the race for overseas territories. He was worried that the British and the French would become more powerful than Germany and so he wanted to acquire more wealth. He sent his armies to different territories and successfully subjugated the people, until they got to Burundi. In the other territories they conquered, they had engaged in armed conflicts with the people or negotiated with their leaders but in Burundi they met with nobody. Whenever the people sighted their approach, they would run deep into the forest where the German army could not go without getting lost. They continued to search for the people but never found them. Eventually, they gave up and returned to Germany.

VOCABULARY

Wann immer - Whenever
Rennen - Race
Erwerben - Acquire
Erobern - Conquer
Unterjochen - Subjugate
Suchen - Search
Eventuell -Eventually
Mehr - More
Andere - Other
Engagiert - Engaged
Niemand - Nobody
Wald - Forest
Ausnutzen - Exploit
Tief - Deep

COMPREHENSION QUESTIONS

Warum schickte Otto von Bismarck seine Armee nach Afrika? Why did Otto von Bismarck send his army to Africa?

Welche Methode wendeten die Menschen in Burundi an, um die deutsche Armee zu besiegen? What method did the people in Burundi employ to defeat the German army?

Vor wem hatte Otto von Bismarck Angst? Who was Otto von Bismarck afraid of?

HISTORICAL NOTE

The German Colonial Empire was made up of overseas colonies, dependencies and territories of the German Empire. Germany joined in the scramble for Africa and claimed most of the uncolonized territories in Africa, making it the third largest colonial empire. It however lost most of its colonies after World War I.

DIE WAHRHEIT DES KRIEGES

Als 1914 der Erste Weltkrieg begann, wollte Hans, ein deutscher Junge, unbedingt in den Krieg ziehen, denn er hatte viele Geschichten über die Tapferkeit der Soldaten gehört. Er meldete sich zur Armee und verließ sein Dorf mit dem Traum, Ruhm zu erlangen. Als er in die Schlacht zog, wurde er mit der Realität des Krieges konfrontiert. Das Schlachtfeld war brutal und blutig, und die Schützengräben, in denen er lag, waren kalt und beängstigend. Er vermisste sein Zuhause, seine Familie und die Tage des Friedens sehr. Inmitten der hoffnungslosen und andauernden Kampfszenen um ihn herum freundete er sich mit anderen Soldaten an, und sie ermutigten sich gegenseitig, trotz der harten Bedingungen und des Tributs, den der Krieg von ihnen forderte, weiterzumachen. 1918 war Deutschland besiegt, aber Hans war nicht traurig. Er war mehr als begierig auf den Frieden und nahm ihn mit Freude an. Er kehrte nach Hause zurück und war dankbar, wieder mit seiner Familie vereint zu sein.

THE TRUTH OF WAR

When World War I started in 1914, Hans, a young German boy, was eager to go to war because he had heard many stories about the bravery of soldiers. He joined the army and left his village filled with dreams of winning glory. As he marched in battle, the reality of war unfolded. The battlefield was brutal with gory scenes and the trenches he laid in were cold and frightening. He missed home, his family, and the days of peace greatly. Amidst the hopeless and continuous scenes of battle around him, he befriended fellow soldiers, and they encouraged each other to keep going despite the harsh conditions and the toll the war took on their spirits. In 1918, Germany was defeated but Hans couldn't be sad. He was more than eager for peace and he embraced it gladly. He returned home, grateful to reunite with his family.

VOCABULARY

Familie - Family

Inmitten von - Amidst

Schauplätze - Scenes

Kolleginnen und Kollegen - Fellow

Ermutigen - Encourage

Traurig - Sad

Geist - Spirit

Befreundet - Befriend

Vereinigen - Unite

Dankbar - Grateful

Umarmen - Embrace

Wirklichkeit - Reality

Eifrig - Eager

Geschichten - Stories

COMPREHENSION QUESTIONS

Warum war Hans vom Krieg begeistert? Why was Hans excited about the war?

Welche Lektionen lernte er während des Krieges? What lessons did he learn during the war?

Was hat Hans in seiner Zeit als Soldat aufrechterhalten? What sustained Hans in his time as a soldier?

HISTORICAL NOTE

Germany led the central powers in World War I, a faction against the Allies. However, it was eventually defeated , partly occupied and forced to pay war reparations. Its colonies were also taken away as well as other territories around its border.

BRAVES HERZ

Nach dem Ersten Weltkrieg herrschte in Deutschland Aufbruchstimmung, und die Menschen sehnten sich nach einer Veränderung. Anna war eine junge Frau, die zu dieser Zeit in einer Fabrik arbeitete. Sie und die anderen Arbeiter leisteten viel Arbeit, bekamen aber nur einen mageren Lohn. Anna war der Entbehrungen und der Ungleichheit überdrüssig und beschloss, etwas dagegen zu unternehmen. Sie hielt eine Versammlung mit den anderen Arbeitern ab, und sie beschlossen, ihre Beschwerden vorzubringen. An einem vereinbarten Tag gingen sie auf die Straße und protestierten gegen ihre ungerechten Arbeitsbedingungen. Sie forderten faire Löhne und bessere Arbeitsbedingungen. Im ganzen Land begannen andere Angestellte und Fabrikarbeiter, ihre Aktionen nachzuahmen, und die Proteste dauerten tagelang an. Im ganzen Land herrschte Stillstand, da die meisten Arbeitnehmer auf die Straße gingen und die Arbeit verweigerten, bis ihre Forderungen erfüllt waren. Schließlich gaben die Arbeitgeber nach und die Regierung griff ein, indem sie günstige Arbeitsgesetze erließ. Anna und ihre Kollegen waren erstaunt darüber, was sie durch ihre Stimme erreichen konnten, und feierten ihren Sieg.

BRAVE HEART

After World War I, Germany was stirring with change and the people clamored for a difference. Anna was a young woman who worked in a factory at the time. She and the other workers did so much work but got meager pay. Tired of the hardship and inequality, Anna decided to do something about this. She held a meeting with the other workers and they resolved to express their grievances. They came out into the streets on an agreed day and protested their unfair working conditions. They demanded fair wages and better working conditions. All around the country, other employees and factory workers started to emulate their actions and the protests went on for days. The country was in a state of lockdown as most workers took to the streets and refused to work until their demands were met. Eventually, the employers gave in and the Government intervened by making favorable labor laws. Anna and her colleagues were amazed at what they were able to achieve by speaking up and celebrated their victory.

VOCABULARY

Härtefall - Hardship
Ändern - Change
Clamor - Clamor
Fabrik - Factory
Karg - Meager
Ungleichheit - Inequality
Aktionen - Actions
nachahmen - Emulate
Ausdrücken - Express
Straßen - Streets
Forderungen - Demands
Löhne - Wages
Bedingungen - Conditions

COMPREHENSION QUESTIONS

War Anna mit ihrer Lebensqualität zufrieden? Was Anna satisfied with her quality of life?

Auf welche Vereinbarung haben sich Anna und ihre Freunde geeinigt? What agreement did Anna and her friends come to?

Wie hat die Regierung die Krise gelöst? How did the government resolve the crisis?

HISTORICAL NOTE

The German Revolution of 1918-1919 took place at the end of World War I. It lasted until November of 1918 and lasted until the adoption of the Weimar Constitution in August 1919. It resulted in the downfall of the German Empire and eventually resulted in the establishment of the Weimar Republic.

DAS LICHT IN UNSEREN HERZEN

Während der Herrschaft der Nazis in Deutschland beherbergte ein alter Schuldirektor, Herr Schmidt, heimlich eine jüdische Familie auf seinem Dachboden. Der junge Hans war sein Nachbar und hatte es eines Tages entdeckt. Hans wollte helfen, aber er hatte keine Ahnung, was er tun sollte, und er hatte auch große Angst. Eines Tages hörte er ein Gespräch mit, das ihm bewusst machte, wie groß die Gefahr für seinen Nachbarn war. Hans nahm seinen Mut zusammen und beschloss, ihm zu helfen. Er brachte Herrn Schmidt und der versteckten Familie spät in der Nacht Essen und Nachrichten. Er spielte mit den kleinen Kindern, Howard und Emily, und brachte ihnen Bücher zum Lesen. Doch je mehr der Konflikt wuchs, desto größer wurden auch die Risiken. Eines Abends klopfte es an die Tür von Herrn Schmidt. Es waren die Soldaten, die Einlass verlangten, da sie Gerüchte über Juden im Haus gehört hatten. Hans, der sich mit seiner Familie im Haus befand, führte sie durch eine Geheimtür in sein Haus. Die Soldaten durchsuchten das Haus gründlich, gingen aber wieder, als sie niemanden fanden.

THE LIGHT IN OUR HEARTS

During the rule of Nazi's in Germany, an old school principal, Mr. Schmidt, secretly sheltered a jewish family in his attic. Young Hans was his neighbor and had discovered it one day. Hans wanted to help out but he had no idea what to do and he was also very afraid. One day, he overheard conversation that made him realize how much danger his neighbor faced. Hans summoned courage and decided to help out. He took food and news to Mr Schmidt and the hidden family late at night. He played with their little children, Howard and Emily and brought them books to read. However, as the conflict grew, the risks also increased. One evening, a knock echoed on Mr. Schmidt's door. It was the soldiers demanding entry as they had heard rumors about jews living in the house. Hans, who was inside with the family, led them through a secret door into his house. The soldiers searched furiously but left when they found no one.

VOCABULARY

Tür - Door
Wütend - Furiously
Innen - Inside
Haus - House
Gefahr - Danger
Hilfe - Help
Alte - Old
Schule - School
Essen - Food
Nachrichten - News
Versteckt - Hidden
Nacht - Night
Nachbarschaft - Neighbor
Konversation - Conversation

COMPREHENSION QUESTIONS

Wie hat Hans die Anwesenheit der jüdischen Familie empfunden? How did Hans feel about the presence of the Jewish family?

Wie hat er Herrn Schmidt geholfen? How did he help Mr. Schmidt?

Warum hat Hans Herrn Schmidt geholfen? Why did Hans help Mr. Schmidt out?

HISTORICAL NOTE

Nazi Germany was a totalitarian regime that made racism and antisemitism a central tenet of its policies. It annexed border territories and invaded Poland, causing World War II. It established a systemic genocide, the Holocaust, which killed 17 million people including 6 million jews.

ZUHAUSE IST, WO DAS HERZ IST

In Eisendorf, einer kleinen Stadt in Deutschland, waren die Auswirkungen des Kalten Krieges deutlich zu spüren. Maria hatte ihr ganzes Leben mit ihrer Familie verbracht und war bei Onkeln, Tanten und Cousinen aufgewachsen. Plötzlich wurde die Berliner Mauer errichtet und trennte sie von ihren Lieben. Ihr Vater, der einst Soldat war, aber zurückkam und seinen Bruder für immer von ihm getrennt vorfand, starb an einem gebrochenen Herzen. Anna trug den Verlust ihrer Lieben mit sich herum, bis eines Abends ein Brief von ihrem Onkel, der hinter der Berliner Mauer verschollen war, vor ihrer Haustür eintraf. Er wünschte sich Freiheit und Wiedervereinigung mit seiner geliebten Nichte. Die Entdeckung, dass ihr Onkel am Leben war und wieder einen Grund zum Glücklichsein hatte, gab Anna Auftrieb. Entschlossen machte sie sich auf eine geheime Reise und überquerte die Grenzen, während sie die Wachposten umging. Schließlich fand sie ihren Onkel. Sie waren wieder glücklich vereint und lebten zusammen, bis die Mauer fiel.

HOME IS WHERE THE HEART LIES

In Eisendorf, a small town in Germany, the effects of the Cold War were deeply felt. Maria had lived all her life with her family, growing up around uncles and aunties and cousins. Suddenly, the Berlin wall was erected, separating her from her loved ones. Her father who was once a soldier but came back to find his brother separated permanently from him died of a broken heart. Anna carried the loss of her loved ones around with her until one evening, a letter arrived at her doorstep from her uncle who had been lost behind the Berlin Wall. He desired freedom and to reunite with his dear niece. Anna was buoyed by the discovery that her uncle was alive and once again had a reason to be happy. Determined, she set out on a covert journey and crossed the borders while dodging watch posts. Finally, she found her uncle. They reunited happily and lived together until the wall eventually came down.

VOCABULARY

Kleine - Small
Effekte - Effects
Filz - Felt
Onkel - Uncle
Cousin - Cousin
Wand - Wall
Errichtet - Erected
Bruder - Brother
Verlust - Loss
Uhr - Watch
Beitrag - Post
Grund - Reason
Verdeckt - Covert
Grenze - Border

COMPREHENSION QUESTIONS

Wie wirkte sich der Kalte Krieg auf Marias Lebensqualität aus? How did the Cold War affect Maria's quality of life?

Was für eine Kindheit hatte Maria? What kind of childhood did Maria have?

Was war Marias höchster Punkt während des Krieges? What was Maria's highest point during the war?

HISTORICAL NOTE

Germany spent the entirety of the Cold War divided into two. West Germany aligned itself with NATO while East Germany aligned with the Warsaw Pact. The Berlin wall was erected as a divider . In 1989, the wall came down and the east and west were reunited in 1990.

DIE EUROPÄISCHE UNION

Als Deutschland der Europäische Union beitrat, beschloss es, den anderen Mitgliedstaaten ein Geschenk zu geben. Es brachte ein Team von Erfindern und klugen Köpfen zusammen, um etwas Spektakuläres zu entwerfen. Mit ihren gemeinsamen Fähigkeiten entwickelten die Erfinder ein sehr effizientes Solarenergiesystem, das Licht spendet, ohne die Umwelt zu schädigen. Deutschland stellte diese Erfindung anderen Ländern als Geschenk zur Verfügung, um den internationalen Zusammenhalt zu fördern. Die Erfinder entwarfen auch Recyclingmaschinen, um Abfälle in ganz Europa zu reduzieren. Die deutschen Beiträge ermutigen andere Länder, ihre Ideen zu teilen, um einen besseren Kontinent für alle zu schaffen.

THE EUROPEAN UNION

Upon joining the European Union, Germany decided to present a gift to the other member states. It brought together a team of inventors and clever thinkers to design something spectacular. With their joint abilities, the inventors developed a super-efficient solar energy system that would give light without harming the environment. Germany made this invention readily available to other countries as a gift and to foster international unity. The inventors also designed recycling machines to reduce waste all around Europe. Germany's contributions encouraged other countries to share their ideas to create a better continent for everyone.

VOCABULARY

Teilen - Share
Abfall - Waste
Geschenk - Present
Team - Team
Klug - Clever
Erstellen - Create
Fördern - Foster
Reduzieren - Reduce
Kontinent - Continent
Mitglied - Member
Gemeinsame - Joint
Fähigkeit - Ability
Energie - Energy
System - System

COMPREHENSION QUESTIONS

Was waren die Geschenke Deutschlands an die Europäische Union? What were Germany's gifts to the European Union?

Was waren die Beweggründe für die Schenkungen? What motivated the act of gifting?

Welche Auswirkungen hatte dies auf die anderen Länder? What effects did this have on the other countries?

HISTORICAL NOTE

The European Union is a political and economic union of 27 member states located in Europe. Relations between France and Germany became important to the inclusion of Western Europe in the European Union.

Conclusion

Learning the basics of any language is difficult, and the German language can feel daunting for many newcomers. With that being said, if you were able to finish all of the lessons in this book, you have built a solid foundation in German.

However, learning a language is a long process that rewards consistency. Even just listening and watching German shows for 30 minutes a day can go a long way in improving your German skills. We sincerely hope that you continue your German language journey with the foundation you have built up and reach your goals, whether that be to understand the basics or speak like a native.

Thank you for choosing our book along your path to German mastery and we hope that you obtained a lot of useful information! If you have any questions, comments, or even suggestions we would love to hear from you by email at Contact@ worldwidenomadbooks.com. We greatly appreciate the feedback and this allows us to improve our books and provide the best language learning experience we can.

Thank you,

Worldwide Nomad Team

Made in the USA
Middletown, DE
27 August 2024